C000263333

A2.

The Search for Old Wirral

A historical guide to Wirral's buildings and sites from Roman times to the Civil War

by

David Randall

With a Foreword by Alan Brack

First published 1984 by Countyvise Limited, 1 & 3 Grove Road, Rock Ferry, Birkenhead, Wirral, Merseyside L42 3XS.
This revised edition published 1993   ISBN 0 907768 61 X

Copyright © David Randall, 1984 and 1993
Photoset and printed by Birkenhead Press Limited, 1 & 3 Grove Road, Rock Ferry, Birkenhead, Merseyside L42 3XS.
Bound by BPCC Wheatons Ltd, Exeter.

In Memory of my Father,
Douglas Sydney Randall,
1917-1974.

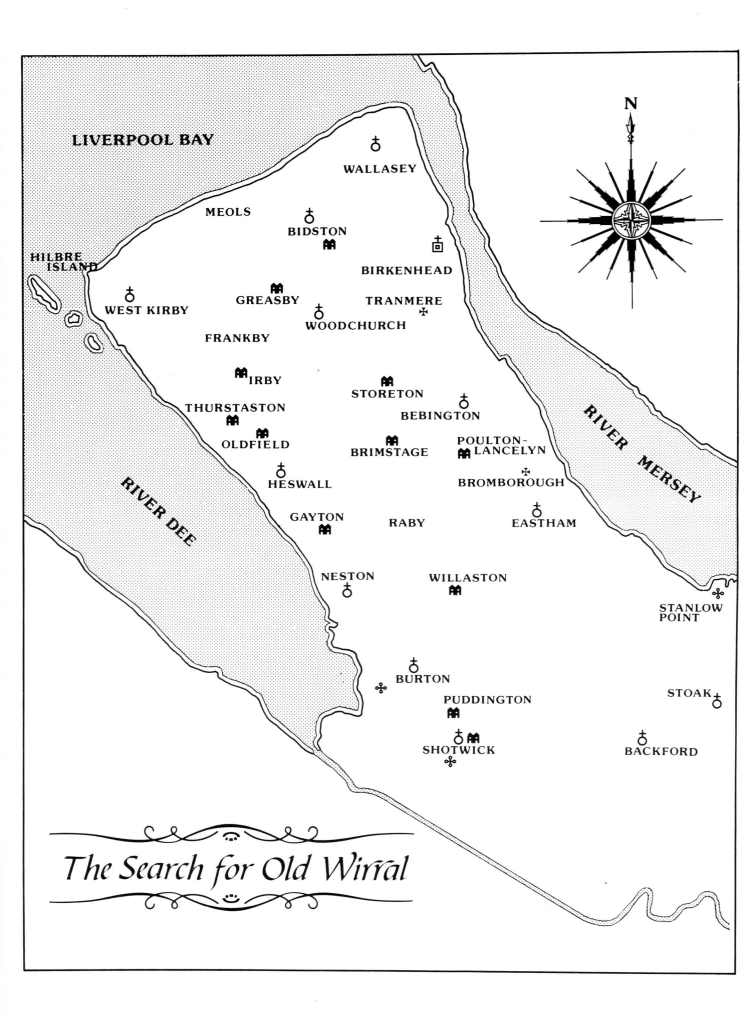

LIVERPOOL BAY

HILBRE
ISLAND

N

MEOLS

WALLASEY

BIDSTON

BIRKENHEAD

WEST KIRBY

GREASBY

TRANMERE

WOODCHURCH

FRANKBY

IRBY

STORETON

THURSTASTON

BEBINGTON

OLDFIELD

BRIMSTAGE

POULTON~
LANCELYN

HESWALL

BROMBOROUGH

RIVER DEE

GAYTON

RABY

EASTHAM

RIVER MERSEY

NESTON

WILLASTON

STANLOW
POINT

BURTON

PUDDINGTON

STOAK

SHOTWICK

BACKFORD

The Search for Old Wirral

The Search for Old Wirral
Map of the principal places mentioned in the text

ᛟᛟ   Manor House or Hall

⚲   Mediaeval Church (with some or all of the structure still standing)

⚲   Religious House

⚜   Scheduled Ancient Monument

⚜   Mediaeval Village Cross

0   1   2   3   4   5 Miles

Fig. 1.
Map of Wirral, showing principal places mentioned in the text. (Drawn by Alan Jones).

Contents

List of Illustrations

PHOTOGRAPHS

1. Overchurch runic stone.
2. Pre-Norman cross fragment (Church of St. Mary and St. Helen, Neston).
3. Pre-Norman cross fragment (Church of St. Mary and St. Helen, Neston).
4. Restored church cross, Bromborough.
5. The Wirral horn.
6. Gayton Mill.
7. Pre-Norman cross fragments (Charles Dawson Brown Museum, West Kirby).
8. Chapel site, Denhall.
9. Cottage at Rock Villa, West Kirby.
10. Old House at Greasby (corner of Mill Lane and Greasby Road).
11. Cruck-built barn (Vineyard Farm, Poulton-Lancelyn).
12. Barn End, Burton.
13. Old roof trusses, Shotwick Lodge Farm.
14. The old house ('Bird's Tenement'), Wallasey.
15. Pensby Hall.
16. Oxton Old Hall.
17. Norman capital (Church of St. Andrew, Bebington).
18. Church tower, Backford (Church of St. Oswald).
19. Tudor arches (Church of St. Andrew, Bebington).
20. The old house ('Bird's Tenement'), Wallasey.
21. Mother Redcap's, Wallasey.
22. Door jambs, Leasowe Castle.
23. Leasowe Castle, from the south-east.
24. Site of Church of St. Hilary, Wallasey, from the south.
25. Norman font (Church of St. Luke, Poulton).
26. The Old Rectory and church tower, Wallasey.
27. Old fireplace, Old Rectory.
28. Ivy Cottage, Saughall Massie.
29. Meols artefacts.
30. Submerged forest at Meols, c.1922.
31. Birkenhead Priory, 1780.
32. Birkenhead Priory, 1727.
33. Chapter house, Birkenhead Priory (interior).
34. Chapter house, Birkenhead Priory (exterior).
35. 13th century doorway, (west range, Birkenhead Priory).
36. Guest Hall, Birkenhead Priory.
37. Western range of Priory.
38. Bidston Village, from the west.
39. Old wall, Bidston Hill.
40. Church Farm, Bidston.
41. West doorway (Church of St. Oswald, Bidston).
42. 'The Lilacs', Bidston c.1910.
43. Yew Tree Farm, Bidston.
44. Bidston Hall, 1665.
45. Bidston Hall, interior.
46. Bidston Hall, exterior.
47. South porch (Church of the Holy Cross, Woodchurch).
48. Lancet window and wheel cross (Church of the Holy Cross, Woodchurch).
49. Mediaeval poppy-head (Church of the Holy Cross, Woodchurch).
50. Tranmere cross.
51. Cottage at Bebington.
52. Norman arcade (Church of St. Andrew, Bebington).
53. Church of St. Andrew, Bebington, from the south-east.
54. East window (Church of St. Andrew, Bebington).
55. Poulton Hall, from the west.
56. Old family chest, Poulton Hall.

LIST OF COLOUR PLATES

PHOTOGRAPHIC NOTE

Except where stated, the photographs were taken specifically for this book by the author using Fujica, Olympus and Praktica equipment. Kodakchrome 25 (colour) and Kodak Pan X (black and white) film was used almost exclusively. Available light was used for all interior shots, typically 25 seconds exposure at f.5.6.

The author would like to thank the following for supplying photographs for reproduction, or granting permission to use certain photographs: The Grosvenor Museum, Chester; The Historic Society of Lancashire and Cheshire; Jim O'Neil; Metropolitan Borough of Wirral, Department of Leisure Services and Tourism (Libraries and Arts Division); The Williamson Art Gallery and Museum, Birkenhead; The Bromborough Society; Ellesmere Port and Neston Borough Council and Unilever PLC.

MAPS, PLANS AND DRAWINGS

Figures

The author wishes to thank the following for permission to reproduce certain plans and drawings: Gill Chitty and the Merseyside Archaeology Society, (Figs. 2,3,4); The Historic Society of Lancashire and Cheshire (T.H.S.L.C.) Figs. 7,8,11; Canon M.H.Ridgway and the Chester Archaeological Society (J.C.A.S.) Figs. 9,13; Cheshire County Council Planning Department and W. Hardman (Fig. 15); Elizabeth and Vaughan Lancaster-Thomas (Fig. 16).

Acknowledgements

A work of this kind owes much to the owners and custodians of Wirral's historic buildings. To all those people who accomodated me so courteously during my travels, who answered my questions and allowed me to photograph their homes, may I extend grateful thanks. I must not forget to mention, too, the numerous clergy who have stood my enquiries and pestering.

It is perhaps invidious to single out individuals but I would like to thank, in particular, June and Roger Lancelyn Green (Poulton Hall), Richard Turner (Thurstaston Hall), Bill Hardman (Ash Tree Farm, Willaston), Jack Pollard (Corner House Farm, Willaston), Mrs. Swift (Neston Church) and Claud Berry (Shotwick Church).

Various 'experts' have been kind enough to comment critically on my text although the final version is my own responsibility. Many of these experts are teachers by profession and I sometimes think that they accept this sort of counselling as an occupational hazard. However, this makes their interest and assistance no less heartening, and I have been overwhelmed by their generosity.

I wish to thank one-time colleague (and boss!) Alan Brack for his help and hospitality. He has cast his experienced and authoritative eye over the final stages of the manuscript and proofs, and also commented on style. Alan and his wife Edith have been very helpful too, with the publishing aspect of book production.

I first met Paul Booth when he interviewed me for the University of Liverpool Institute of Extension Studies, 'Diploma in Local History' course in 1977. I am happy to say that, with this book, we renewed our acquaintance. Paul has given me words of advice and encouragement, freely providing his own unpublished material, and commented critically on parts of Chapter I and Chapter VI.

Elizabeth Davey has kindly commented on Chapter IV and looked at the proofs. Glenys Lloyd-Morgan, at the Grosvenor Museum, Chester, guided me through the Meols antiquities and provided her own unpublished material and Gill Chitty was my guide at the Sites and Monuments Record, Merseyside County Museums. The latter two ladies also helped me with my section on the early settlement of Wirral.

Susan Craggs (Wallasey), Alf Jones (Bromborough) and Jim O'Neil (Greasby) all provided useful advice.

Oliver Bott and Rhys Williams, in the Cheshire County Council Planning Department, helped me with conservation and archaeology respectively.

I would like to thank, also, Cliff Thornton at the Williamson Art Gallery and Museum in Birkenhead, for his assistance, Ron Sumner of The Wirral Society and Alan Jones and Shirley Robinson for their splendid art-work. The staff at Wallasey and Birkenhead reference libraries, and the Cheshire Record Office, helped locate material.

John Emmerson and his wife Pat have shown much interest and faith in the book from the start. Christine Adamson has supplied a map and given me much encouragement during the final stages of the project. Finally, allow me to record my gratitude to my sister Carolyn. For the past two years she has tolerated a house full of files and books, and a bathroom frequently filled with dripping prints. I think she will be as relieved as I am to see this work in print!

Foreword

In the many books that have been written about the Wirral Peninsula down the years it would not be unreasonable to presume that everything that is known about it has by now been committed to print. It is not a vast area after all and all that would seem to be needed is a periodic updating both for posterity's sake and the enlightenment of rising generations. Yet David Randall has struck a new vein. He has realised that most of the published accounts of the growth of Wirral have concentrated in the main on its development following the introduction of steam ferries across the Mersey. So he has chosen to deal with the millenium beginning with the coming of the Romans and ending with the Civil War — and many readers will be surprised to learn just how much of interest there is to relate. But he does not always stay his hand at the 17th century; where the story demands it he brings it up to date. Moreover, he has given us the novelty of what he calls 'a sort of glorified guidebook' and has borne in mind that some readers will not be content just to sit at home and read about events but will want to go out and examine the evidence for themselves. From that aspect, too, it will surely be an invaluable aid to schools and students of our local history. And wherever he has been he has taken a camera with him, with the result that there has never been a book on Wirral so copiously illustrated. If we allow that every picture tells a thousand words then this is indeed a comprehensive work.

David Randall has an honours degree in history and with the eye of the trained historian he has been into almost every building he describes, trodden old footpaths and byways, examined old earthworks, looked at relics in the museums and in private hands, delved into historic documents and pored over old records. The diligence of his research is plain to see from the wealth of references given at the end of each chapter.

While the author does not claim to have discovered anything really new during his two-year quest, nor indeed anything which dramatically upsets the history of Wirral in general he does go into great detail so that even those who consider themselves experts will surely learn something they did not know. I can see it being seized upon by people setting examination papers and quizzes or being used simply to settle arguments in pubs. Did you know, for example, that Wirral was once known as 'Kilgwry'? Or that Wallasey was at one time 'Kirkby in Waley'? Or that the gentry of Wirral at one period were some of the biggest crooks in the land, indulging in raids, burglaries, rapes, poisonings and prison breaking? I must not spoil the reading of the book by giving too much away.

The approach has been to divide the peninsula into its main components (which are not those determined by the Local Boundaries Commission) . . . Wallasey/North Wirral; Birkenhead/Bebington; the villages; Deeside and Eastham/South Wirral . . . and then to give a general introduction to each area followed by detailed descriptions of the buildings and sites of interest and the stories behind them. The last chapter is an account of what has and is being done to preserve Wirral's past. We are told of the Green Belt policy and the Conservation Areas and what steps have been taken towards the preservation and restoration of buildings of some historical significance. Much of this information is normally only available to those who go to the trouble of digging it out of planning departments and libraries so to that extent it will serve as a ready reference.

The true purpose of a Foreword, said the late Lord Birkett, the eminent judge, is not always understood; it is to do no more than introduce the author and commend his work to the attention of the reading public. 'The writer of a Foreword,' he continued, 'must perform his task with truth and candour and unless he can do this he has no right to undertake the duty at all.' My own credentials are that I have been writing about Wirral, *inter alia,* for more years than I care to remember so that I am interested both in the subject matter and the way it is put down on paper. In this respect David Randall succeeds on both counts. I have said enough to indicate the interest his book has aroused in me; as to the writing, he has an easy readable style which one does not often meet with in historians. More importantly, he has shown that anyone else who wants to go in search of old Wirral for themselves will be surprisingly and richly rewarded.

ALAN BRACK

Preface

My awareness of the Wirral peninsula was first kindled during numerous schoolday cycle rides; visits to Thornton Hough, Burton and Raby stimulated my interest in the local landscape. In 1981 I attended a half-day school given by Paul Booth and Elizabeth Davey, under the aegis of the University of Liverpool Institute of Extension Studies. After this discussion of 'Medieval Wirral : The Buildings and the People,' I was convinced that there was a need for a comprehensive guide to Wirral's early buildings and sites.

One of my main aims in writing this book has been to bring together a variety of material relating to Wirral, and to make this sometimes obscure research available to the general reader. I therefore make no high claims for historical originality although, if my debt to earlier writers is obvious, I hope that my own views and researches will be apparent.

Historical synthesis is no bad thing if it encourages and stimulates further study, and popularisation is necessary to make history accessible and relevant to the modern world.

This is, then, a sort of glorified guide book, both to Wirral's historic buildings and sites and to the sources for Wirral's history. Although it is written for the general reader, I hope the references might make it useful to a school student.

In 1974, for administrative purposes, the peninsula was split into two counties, Merseyside and Cheshire. For the purposes of this book I have considered that part of the peninsula north of the Shropshire Union Canal approximating to the old administrative area, the Hundred of Wirral. There are some noticeable omissions, I have not, for example, dealt with places like Ellesmere Port, Thornton Hough or Port Sunlight because they are essentially modern, purpose-built, villages.

For the chapter headings — for convenience — I have followed modern boundaries and beg forgiveness if this 'perambulation' approach seems rather familiar. The chapter titled 'Villages of Wirral' is meant to reflect the broad central strip running through Wirral and now designated Green Belt.

I have tried to keep technical terms to the minimum; there are though, several good architectural and historical 'dictionaries.' (See Appendix III and Bibliography). Finally, I have included Appendices II and III and a Select Bibliography in the hope that this will help you in your own search for old Wirral.

DAVID RANDALL
Wallasey,
September 1983.

Preface to 1993 Edition

It is now nearly ten years since the original publication of *The Search For Old Wirral*. Although building use and ownership has changed during this period the nub of my story remains the same. My original aim to publicize Wirral's early history and encourage further study remains also.

Since the book's first publication, the Archaeological Survey of Merseyside has been integrated into the Field Archaeology Section at Liverpool Museum, and work has continued apace.

Several Roman and sub-Roman sites in the Irby/Thurstaston areas have been identified and explored. At Thurstaston, Roman brooches, several coins (dating from the 1st Century BC to the Third Century AD) and an Anglo-Saxon brooch of 6th Century origin indicate the probable continuity of settlement at this particular site.

Other significant discoveries include the mediaeval well at Irby thought to be the "Londymere" mentioned in mediaeval boundary records. The *Journal of the Merseyside Archaeology Society*, Volume 7(Liverpool,1991) provides a useful summary of fieldwork and research in the 1980's with appropriate references and the first volume of the *Victoria County History of Cheshire* (ed . B.E.Harris and A.T.Thacker), published in 1987, deals with the Roman, Anglo-Saxon and Domesday period.

The study of local history is very much one to be undertaken 'on the doorstep' and in this respect there have been several interesting finds such as the uncovering of an old sandstone inglenook fireplace during restoration work at Church Farm, Bidston and, in 1988, the discovery of the datestone from Pool Hall built into a garden seat at a house in Neston.

My final chapter on conservation is particularly relevant. When I wrote in 1984, the local conservation blueprints for Wirral were the *Merseyside Green Belt Subject Plan* and the *Policy for Rural Cheshire*. They have been incorporated in the *Wirral Unitary Development Plan* (UDP) and the Ellesmere Port and Neston *Local Plan*. Both preserve the concept of green belt and promote the idea of urban renewal and, for Wirral Borough, a further seven conservation areas have been proposed.

In addition, the local planning authorities may impose conditions on developers to ensure the preservation and investigation of archaeological sites. The UDP listed forty such sites of national, regional or local importance where planning applications would be refused if the site or its setting was not preserved.

Green issues have become a vital (and political) issue in the 1980's and '90s and if we are to preserve Wirral's countryside and its environmental heritage we need also to enhance the urban centres. This will attract people back to the towns for amenities and dwelling places and reverse the trend that began in the 1920's :the migration of population away from the towns as road networks developed and the use of personal and public transport increased. In this way the green belt concept will be protected.

New building in the urban areas should be sympathetic to the local scene and complement existing architecture; it should be user-friendly, well-designed and durable. I stray here a little from the historical narrative that is essentially *The Search For Old Wirral* but only by being mindful of the future can we appreciate and consolidate the past.

DAVID RANDALL
Neston,
June 1993.

ACKNOWLEDGEMENTS: I wish to thank Jim O'Neil for his assistance with this edition, Rob Philpott of Liverpool Museum for supplying unpublished material, and Rob Burns of Wirral Borough Council for help with conservation.

Chapter 1

An Introduction to Wirral

(i) WIRRAL FROM ROMAN TIMES TO THE NORMAN CONQUEST

When the Romans arrived in Chester, Wirral would have presented a bleak and barren prospect. It was an area of heath, scrub and woodland with a scattering of homesteads clustered around the sandstone outcrops. The northern coastline would have extended further seawards than at present, and the old shoreline of the Dee would have run close to latter-day Neston, Burton and Shotwick. To the south were the marshes of the Gowy valley, and to the east a narrow channel now known as the Mersey. (The name Wirral first appears in the Anglo-Saxon Chronicle (895) and is said to derive from *wir* meaning myrtle and *heal* meaning corner or angle. Before this time, the pre-Roman tribe the Cornovii called the district *Kilgwry*.)

During most of the Roman period Chester was occupied by the Twentieth Legion Valeria Victrix who used it as a base to control the native population of North Wales and the surrounding region. The presence of this army may have stimulated industry, trade and agriculture in the immediate area, but there is very little evidence that the Romans actually penetrated into Wirral. They may have been hampered by woodland and marshes, to the east and to the north-west.

One writer has suggested that Wirral may have been a starting-off point for expeditions to subdue North Wales and Anglesey. This is based on a reference by the chronicler Tacitus in his *Annals,* book XIV; 'Flat bottomed boats were built to contend with the shifting shallows, and these took the infantry across.' However it is mere speculation to suggest that this 'depot' was near Chester or the Dee Estuary. [1]

The Romans are, of course, associated in the popular imagination with the beginnings of urban life and a market economy, and the building of roads. Chester was, however, first and foremost a legionary fortress.

The evidence for the Roman occupation of the peninsula is largely based on single-coin and metalwork finds, coin hoards and various glass and pottery items. [2] Some writers believe that if these finds do not indicate a settlement of some sort, then there must have been a lot of careless people in earlier times. As far as the Roman coins are concerned, some may be collectors' pieces and might not originate from this area.

I have dealt with the Meols artefacts in greater detail in Chapter II, but it is worth emphasising here that many of the finds were badly documented and recorded in the nineteenth-century. We will never know, for example, whether some were found *in situ* or whether they were washed out to the beach. [3] There is also the absence of the metalwork that one would normally associate with a military outpost. Elsewhere in Wirral, there is an absence of pottery finds - so typical of Roman sites - with the notable exception of Hilbre Island. [4] There are finds of Roman tiles, sherds and pottery fragments from Meols in the collections of Liverpool Museum.

Several Romano-British objects have turned up since 1981 as a result of controlled 'treasure hunting' in fields at Thurstaston. These finds, together with aerial evidence, suggest that this site may reveal a substantial sub-Roman settlement. [5]

The evidence for Roman roads in Wirral is better. We are still not certain about the routes of the roads, even though local historians have attempted to analyse these on the basis of straight lane alignments, field names and mediaeval boundary records. [6]

It seems likely that a road once connected Chester (Northgate) to Birkenhead, with another branch to Meols. In 1960 excavations were made by Mr. K.E. Jermy at a point to the east of Street Hey Lane, near the junction with the B5133 road from Hooton to Willaston.[7] A ridge was discovered just inside the hedge and raised above ground level, and this was taken to be the mound (or agger) of the road. At a depth of 19 inches a single, continuous layer of cobbles up to five inches in size were found placed on a sandy layer, some two inches thick immediately above the natural clay. There was, though, no evidence of the gravel layer which would usually provide the actual road surface. Furthermore, no definite dating evidence was discovered.

Some authorities believe that this was part of a road which connected Chester, via Mollington, Ledsham, Poulton-Lancelyn (where a 'Roman' surface was discovered at Vineyard Farm during drainage repairs) and Bebington, to Birkenhead. Its northerly extension, from Hargrave to Old Bidston Road in Birkenhead, was referred to in mediaeval records as Blake Street. Ultimately, it may have terminated at Bridge-End, at the junction of the present Bridge Street, Freeman Street and Marcus Street, where in 1850 a so-called 'Roman' bridge of 'solid oak beams' was discovered during excavations for a railway bridge. [8]

The 'western' route from Chester to Meols — if it existed — is unestablished apart from a tentative excavation at Greasby in 1964 which revealed a surface similar to that at Willaston.[9] Philip Sulley in his book *The Hundred of Wirral* (1889) was convinced that a military road ran from Chester to Shotwick, via Little Saughall and Kingswood Lane.[10] W. Thompson Watkin, writing in 1886, mentioned submerged 'Roman' roads at Blacon Point and off the coast at Neston.[11]

Some old lanes in Wirral have undoubtedly been mis-interpreted and mis-named. Roman Road in Storeton probably originated as a mediaeval pack-horse track and Kirkup (now Kirket) Lane in Bebington probably had a similar function.

The Roman legions had withdrawn from Britain by the early fifth-century and, with the possible exception of isolated areas like Wallasey, successive English settlers colonised Chester and Wirral. The strong Celtic influence in the peninsula is indicated by place-names and church dedications. Wallasey may have been the refuge of Welshmen, Landican suggests the church enclosure of Tegan, a little known Welsh saint. An Irish element is present in the name Noctorum.

On the basis of a sixth-century book written by a British monk, Gildas, it seems that the native Britons appealed to the Romans for help against barbarous Germanic tribes who had broken away from the Roman army.[12] When this help was not forthcoming, they appealed to the Saxons. However, instead of providing assistance, the invited immigrants actually ravaged the whole country. The Venerable Bede described these invaders as Saxons, from Germany, Angles from Scandinavia, and Jutes from Norway.[13]

One of the main characteristics in the history of those early English kingdoms established by the immigrants, is the clear distinction between those people north and south of the Humber; the history of the northern Anglian settlement, and large-scale colonisation in Wirral, really begins with Aethelfrith's victory against the Welsh at Chester about 616.

Archaeological evidence does not contradict Gildas' colourful account but it does show that the Anglo-Saxons and native Britons were not necessarily always in violent conflict. It is wrong to assume that the Romans suddenly departed to be replaced by a wholly alien culture. It is highly likely that Romano-British communities and Anglo-Saxon pagan settlers were living side by side. The ancient settlement at Meols is often given as an example of continuity from Roman times to the fourteenth-century.

The majority of existing place-names in Wirral are of Anglo-Saxon origin. The *ton,* as in Prenton, Storeton and Bebington, signifies an enclosed farmstead while *ham,* as in Eastham and Ledsham, refers to a manor or homestead. An absence of Anglian clearance names, such as *ley,* indicates that much of the Wirral landscape may have been open heath and arable land by the seventh century.[14]

The so-called Overchurch Stone, now in the Grosvenor Museum at Chester, is the finest example of pre-Scandinavian remains in Wirral. It is the first runic inscription to be found in Cheshire and is indeed rare in Europe.

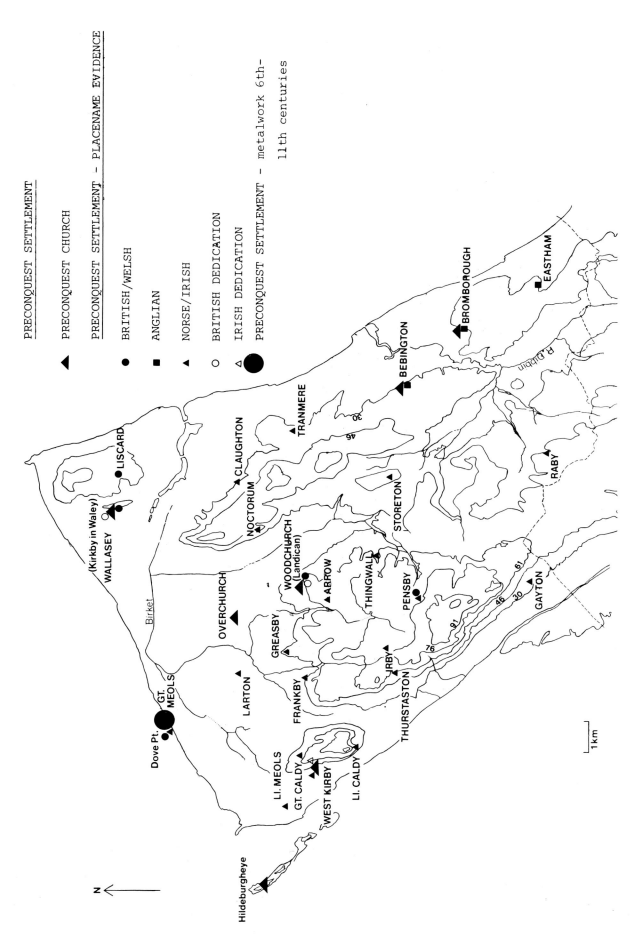

Fig. 2.
Distribution of Pre-Conquest sites and finds (North Wirral) from G. Chitty, 'Wirral Rural Fringes Survey Report', Journal of the Merseyside Archaeology Society, *Vol. 2, (Liverpool, 1978, reprint 1980).*

1.
Overchurch runic stone. Courtesy Grosvenor Museum, Chester.

The stone was discovered in the summer of 1887 when the small, whitewashed church at Upton was being dismantled.[15] It may well have been a horizontal tombstone of the ninth-century and is inscribed with interlaced serpents and runes. The ancient characters have been translated, 'The people erected (this) monument. Pray for Aethelmund's soul.' Although an Aethelmund is mentioned in the Anglo-Saxon Chronicle for 800 A.D. there were probably others by that name, and we will probably never be sure about the subject of the Overchurch dedication.

The Viking raids in England began in the ninth-century. By 879, of the four independent kingdoms which had existed at the middle of the century, only Wessex survived. Most of England had become subject to the Danelaw and the Danegeld, a sort of bribe money paid by the native inhabitants to keep the Danes at bay.

It is fair to say that, until quite recently, the Vikings - or Norsemen - have received a bad press. The traditional view that they were concerned almost exclusively with rape, pillage and plunder is largely based on the writings of contemporary chroniclers. These monks were, not suprisingly, rather biased as it was the monasteries and churches that suffered most at the hands of the Viking raiders.

Recent research presents a different, and more satisfying, picture. This was a period of social and economic development and, as we shall see, significant artistic achievement. [16]

Historically, the Norse invasion of Wirral began in the early tenth-century when Ingimund and his men arrived from Dublin having previously been driven away from Anglesey. This evidence is largely based on the so-called *Three Fragments,* first published in Ireland in 1860 and supposedly based on a copy of a seventeenth-century manuscript.[17] Aethelflaed of Mercia subsequently granted Ingimund land 'near Chester'.

The Norse settlement is indicated by the large number of Scandinavian place-names, especially in the northern half of the peninsula. A number of villages have the element *by,* denoting a farmstead or dwelling, as in Frankby and Pensby. Raby - the village at the boundary - may mark the southern tip of Norse territory. Greasby (Anglo-Saxon, *Gravesberie*) is an interesting example of an English settlement taken over by the Scandinavians. The Irish element is reflected in place-names such as Arrowe (small cottage) and Irby (farmstead of the Irish).

Unlike the Danes, the Norwegians achieved their settlements by gradual - and one assumes peaceful - infiltration, often in undesirable areas. [18] This gradual cultural assimilation is reflected in the art of the period, and especially the carved stones. New kinds of decoration were introduced alongside traditional English motifs, and new forms of ornamentation were developed. In addition, individual artists and workshops were established outside of monastic patronage. [19]

2.
Pre-Norman cross fragment (Church of St. Mary and St. Helen, Neston).

In Wirral, a series of pieces combine English, Scandinavian and Irish features. The Scandinavians introduced a secular element to English sculpture; cross fragments at Neston, for example, show two warriors fighting and and two men wrestling. Another piece at Neston shows a priest holding a satchel - typically Irish in influence. A dramatic innovation was the hogback, inspired by the building - shaped stones of Anglo-Saxon England, and probably used as a grave cover.

The ring-head type of cross - as opposed to the wheel-head cross (an example of which exists at Woodchurch) - is almost wholly confined to the coastal lands of Cumberland, Cheshire, Flintshire and Anglesey. Of the 'Chester' type, the ends of the arms of the cross projected beyond the circle like ears. [20] Examples have been found at Bromborough, and Hilbre which is now held by the Grosvenor Museum, Chester.

Although these surviving fragments of early mediaeval sculpture may look drab and uninteresting to the modern eye, we must remember that these pieces would have originally been brightly painted.

The Charles Dawson Brown Museum, housed in the old school-room to the south of St. Bridget's, West Kirby, is a fascinating and little known collection of early Christian monuments. Open by appointment only, the museum contains a splendid example of a hogback together with pre-Norman cross fragments, mediaeval grave slabs and assorted masonry from the West Kirby district. Much of the material was recovered during the 1869-70 restoration of the church.

The Neston stones (including the lintel removed from the belfry) are now displayed within the church, resting on specially made timber stands so that they can be viewed from all sides.

Apart from sculpture, the Norse settlers also left certain administrative institutions. On the eve of the Norman Conquest (1066), and with the exception of the Danish shires of north-east Mercia, every county south of the Mersey and Humber was divided into hundreds. The term hundred may refer to the quantity of land rateable to the Danegeld, that is roughly 100 hides.

The old hundred of Wirral also included the townships of Upton, Picton, Wervin, Mickle Trafford and Guilden Sutton. As part of Cheshire, it was given by William I to the Norman earls of Chester and remained separate from the crown until 1237 when Henry III repossessed the earldom.

The Hundred Court of Wirral may have originated at the 'Thing', traditionally associated with Cross Hill (by the junction of Barnston Road and Holmwood Drive) in Thingwall. This was a primitive form of government, where decisions were confirmed by a symbolic show of weapons. A more likely meeting-place is a

3.
Pre-Norman cross fragment (Church of St. Mary and St. Helen, Neston).

4.
Restored church cross, Bromborough.

23

central spot such as Willaston, especially as this village gave its name to the hundred in the Middle Ages. Some Cheshire hundreds derive their name from prominent objects such as a stone or hill; this has led some writers to describe the so-called 'Wirral Stone' (at the junction of Hadlow Road and the Chester High Road) as the assembly point. A more acceptable explanation for this stone is given in Chapter IV.

The Hundred Court had both civil and criminal jurisdiction and, until the eleventh-century, handled ecclesiastical suits. It had no power over the forest of Wirral. After 1237 the reeve, or bailiff, collected the profits of the court (which ultimately went to the king) and supervised the administration of the crown estates. [21]

After the Norman Conquest, the importance of the Hundred Court declined and by the reign of Henry III there was the use of quarter sessions, itinerant justices and trial by jury. The court became a purely local tribunal devoted to the collection of small debt and regulating local privileges. It sat until 1856 when an Act of Parliament transferred all pending actions and suits to the County Court.

(ii) THE NORMANS, THE DOMESDAY BOOK AND THE ADMINISTRATION OF CHESHIRE

At the time of the Norman Conquest (1066), and with the accession of William I, only a few townships were left in the possession of their previous owners and these mainly belonged to the Church. The remainder were divided amongst William's warriors. These great barons did not reside in Wirral but left their estates in the hands of retainers.

William I commissioned the Domesday Book in 1086, a national survey which formed the basis of a tax assessment. Commissioners visited most parts of the country, and jurors in each hundred had to submit a return covering land holding, ownership and value. The survey was not merely a taxation document, but an inquiry into the king's territory. Quite simply, William wanted to know exactly what he had conquered. [22]

The survey throws light upon the organisation of Wirral under feudalism, the hierarchical system by which land was held from an overlord. All estates were held from somebody else and the ultimate land owner was, of course, the king who exercised his powers in Cheshire through the Earl of Chester.

Of the 51 Wirral manors enumerated in the Domesday record, the Earl or his tenants held 42, the Abbey of St. Werburgh 8 and the Bishop of Chester 1. The first Norman Earl of Chester, Hugh Lupus, held Trafford, Edelaue (thought to be represented by the present Hadlow in Willaston), Upton, Stanney and Eastham, which was by far the largest of the Wirral manors accounting for one fifth of the whole hundred.

Hugh's cousin, and commander-in-chief, Robert de Rodelent (Rhuddlan) held Mollington, Leighton, Thornton, Gayton, Heswall, Thurstaston, Caldy, Meols and Wallasey. William Malbedeng (Malbank) was the greatest of all tenants in Cheshire, with over forty manors, and in Wirral these included Saughall, Landican, Thingwall and Noctorum. William Fitz-Nigel, the Constable of Chester, held Capenhurst, Barnston and parts of Neston and Raby; Walter de Vernon held Ness, Ledsham and Prenton and Hamo de Mascy (Massey) of Dunham Massey received Puddington.

In addition to supplying us with a very clear picture of land ownership before and after the Conquest, the Domesday survey also allows us to make a reasonable assessment of population and the amount of land under cultivation.

Only three Wirral manors included woodland in their returns - Prenton, Tranmere and Mollington - and this is usually taken to indicate extensive forest clearance from Roman times. [23]

One of the frustrating aspects of the Domesday document is the omission of certain villages and the inclusion of unusual names. We can only assume that if a township was not listed, either it did not exist or it was included under a larger manor. Bidston, Claughton and Frankby, for example, may have come under Eastham.

The manor of Edelaue has now been identified with Hadlow in Willaston (on the basis of field-name evidence) and Sumreford has been taken for Tranmere.

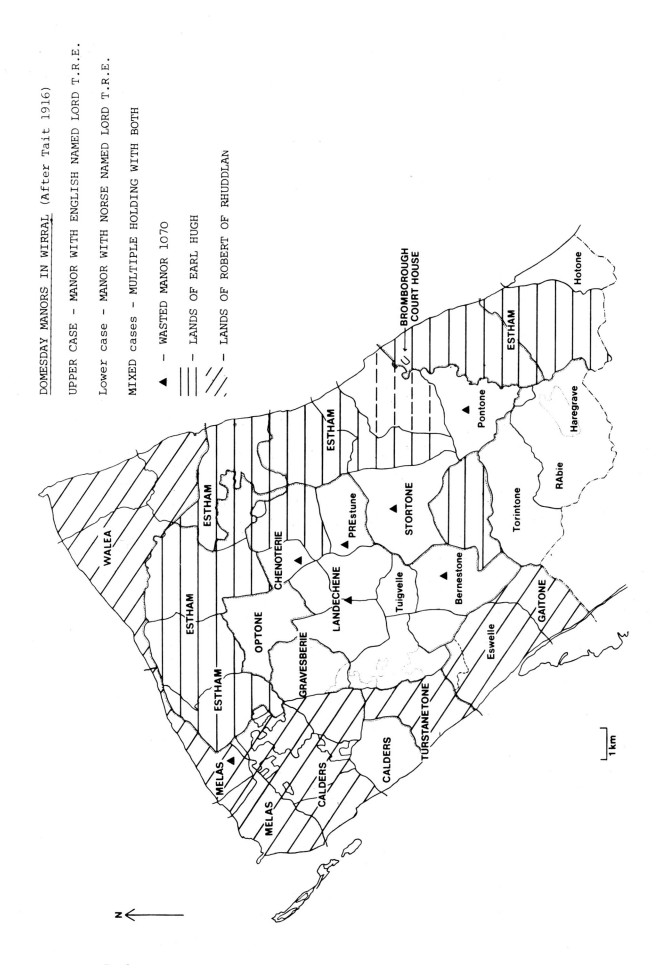

Fig. 3.
Domesday manors in North Wirral from G.Chitty, 'Wirral Rural Fringes Survey Report',
Journal of the Merseyside Archaeological Society, *Vol.2, (Liverpool, 1978, reprint 1980).*

Some townships were obviously misplaced in the survey. Puddington was listed under Nantwich hundred and it has now been convincingly argued that Burton-in-Wirral appeared under Eddisbury (south) hundred. [24]

Only a handful of priests are mentioned for Wirral, although we know from other evidence that many pre-Conquest churches existed. [25]

In Anglo-Saxon times, Cheshire was merely part of Mercia and, in terms of race and culture, was a disorganised region. It began to emerge as a separate territorial entity after the death of Alfred (901), when Mercia was divided into administrative districts called shires. During the tenth-century, Cheshire - or Chester shire - became a financial and administrative area for the support of Chester *burh*, or fortified town.

The Normans called the shires counties, and during their rule Cheshire became a buffer zone to safeguard the Welsh border and control the north-west. This military function had probably been exercised since Roman times.

In the Middle Ages, Cheshire enjoyed extraordinary status amongst English counties. The earls of Chester exercised almost regal powers, issuing their own charters, making their own laws and levying their own taxes.

Some historians have argued that William I consciously and deliberately created Chester as a county palatine in 1071, mainly for strategic reasons. Other writers, following Geoffrey Barraclough's article of 1952, believed that it was only after Cheshire was annexed to the crown in 1237 that the earldom became a county with full palatinate jurisdiction.

Barraclough demonstrated that the power and importance of the earls during the Norman period - their ambition and shrewd political sense - rested upon their extensive land interests *outside* Cheshire, rather than on any special status within the county. [26] There were strict limitations on the earls' power in Cheshire, especially with reference to the church.

In relation to Chester, the term *comes palacii,* meaning an area enjoying royal privileges, was first used officially in 1297. The term 'palatinate' did not become commonly accepted in England until the fifteenth-century. Under Richard II (1377-98) the county palatine of Chester became a source of both men and revenue and the famous Cheshire bodyguard formed the backbone of the king's government. In 1397, as a token of his esteem and gratitude, Richard made Cheshire into a principality. [27]

Ultimately, the semi-feudal palatinate left Cheshire with an antiquated administrative system and contributed to the breakdown of law and order. For most of the fourteenth-century, the county was almost completely excluded from the direct control of royal government due to the wardship of the king's eldest son. And all this time Wirral was remote from the centre of authority. [28]

The semi-regal status of the earldom led to the establishment of separate administrative organisations. The chief administrator was the justiciar, who appointed officials, leased out lands and offices and, either he or his deputy, presided over the county court.

The chamberlain was the county's chief financial officer although by the fifteenth-century the sheriff was rising in importance. He accounted for rents and maintained public order.

On a local basis, law and order was regulated by the sergeants of the peace, accompanied by their assistants or *bedells.* [29] They perambulated each hundred, noting all offences and abuses, and the cost of their upkeep was carried by the local community in a payment known as *puture.*

During the later Middle Ages this payment was increasingly made in money rather than in kind, and this led to frequent claims of harassment and extortion by the officials. [30]

The Master-Foresters had overall control, and a right to certain privileges, within a forest.

Under the early Tudors, a policy of administrative assimilation was carried out. In the reign of Henry VIII (1509-47) a series of measures brought Cheshire into line with other counties, and in 1540 a final blow was dealt to Cheshire's traditional independence when parliamentary subsidies were imposed. Finally, in 1543, the county and city of Chester were granted representation in parliament.

(iii) THE FOREST OF WIRRAL

The term forest when applied to Wirral often conjures up the image of a peninsula covered in dense woodland and beasts. In the Middle Ages the term merely referred to a large area of open ground subject to a special code, the forest law, which was rapidly introduced to England after the Conquest.

At the time of the Domesday survey, Wirral was not heavily wooded. Tradition states that the third Earl of Chester, Ranulf of Meschines (1120-29), converted the area to forest as a sort of retributive measure: the natives resented Norman methods of organisation and the loss of their traditional customs. Wirral did not become a royal forest until the late thirteenth-century.

Ostensibly, the forest laws aimed to determine the forest boundaries and to preserve the woods and wildlife for the sport of the king. Increasingly, however, the profits of jurisdiction and timber were exploited by the king and harnessed to the royal coffers.

According to fourteenth-century documents, the people of Wirral claimed that the presence of the forest - both the beasts and the bureaucracy - was an imposition. Those living near or in the forest could not own greyhounds, their dogs had to be lawed (that is the claws had to be removed) and grazing and cultivation was restricted. [31]

Perhaps even more onerous was the shadow of officialdom. In order to maintain and preserve the forests, certain officers were appointed by the earl to investigate offences and to survey damaged hedges and trees. [32]

The chief forester appointed by Ranulf was possibly Alan Sylvester who also received, in connection with the office, the manors of Puddington and Storeton. The Wirral Horn, now in the possession of the Earl of Cromer, probably became the symbol of this royal grant (c. 1129-39). [33]

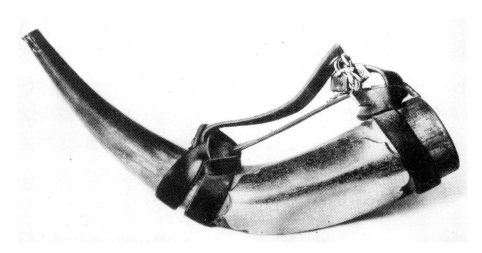

5.
The Wirral horn. Courtesy Historic Society of Lancashire and Cheshire.

The Master-Forester claimed certain rights and privileges, including puture, timber, beasts, and even bees. Exploitation and extortion by these officials was rife, and in the trailbaston court of 1353 William Stanley was found guilty of extracting money from certain townships, including Bidston. [34] In return he had allowed them to keep their sheep in the woods at the time of fawning.

There is no doubt that the Master-Forester's henchmen - known as sergeants of the peace - abused their official position. In 1353 John Lasselles was found guilty of various crimes committed in Wallasey. He stole a boat at Seacombe, assaulted a man at Liscard and tied him to a post, he forced Henry Litherland's servant to enter his service and assaulted another man at Poulton, firing arrows at him. [35]

In that same court it was claimed that the foresters of Wirral repeatedly terrorised the common people of Wirral, while exercising their official duties. Furthermore, they issued threats so that the people would not dare to complain about the oppression. [36]

The foresters' claim to subsistence, or puture, was a constant burden on the community. It was said that the officials went round on horseback, contrary to Earl Ranulf III's charter (granted 1194-1208) which specifically stated that the six Wirral foresters (excluding the Master and his deputy) should go round on foot.

As a result of this, the foresters destroyed crops and increased the expenses of their reluctant hosts. [37]

Perhaps the biggest burden for the people of Wirral were the fines imposed for 'offences' in the forest. In 1347, for example, they were fined £184 although this was subsequently scaled down. Ten years later, fines for 'new ploughings' - the destruction of wood and the building of houses and windmills within the forest - totalled £1,000. Even in 1384, eight years after Wirral had been disafforested, a fine of 600 marks was levied on the hundred by Richard II. [38]

The financial implication of forest law, rather than its criminal function, is best reflected in the events of 1353. A general eyre and trailbaston (or court of itinerant justices) was ordered upon the visit of Edward, the Black Prince, to Cheshire. It was then cancelled because it was claimed that Chester had a county court. In the meantime, a cash payment of 5,000 marks was extracted in lieu. [39]

Ultimately, Edward bowed to the pressure of petition. In 1376 Wirral was removed from forest law. Possibly, the Prince feared the loss of military support; Cheshire archers and gentry had accompanied him to Gascony in 1369. On a local basis, he may have wanted to break the Mafia-style organisation of the Stanleys. More likely, as Paul Booth of Liverpool University has argued, the act was a sort of religious insurance policy. [40] Edward may have wanted to secure his salvation by a good work. He died before the charter could be confirmed, and it was subsequently issued by his father, Edward III.

Despite the disafforestation, small enclosed deer parks remained at Shotwick, Puddington, Neston, Hooton and Bidston. They would have supplied both sport and savouries. In 1363 the chamberlain of Chester was ordered to take 100 harts and 100 bucks in the forest of Wirral, and have them preserved and despatched to Bordeaux. [41]

Before Wirral was released from forest law, the clergy were particularly active in the forest as they claimed exemption from the restrictions. Among those convicted in the forest proceedings of the thirteenth and fourteenth centuries were the Prior of Birkenhead, the rector of Woodchurch, the vicar of Backford and the Abbot of Chester.

There was certainly no love lost between William Stanley and the Abbot of Chester. Stanley claimed that in November 1360 the Abbot's steward grievously threatened him and came into his area of jurisdiction with at least 13 armed men, much to the terror of the local people. [42]

(iv) POPULATION AND THE ECONOMY

At best, the Domesday Book can offer only a rough guide to population in the late eleventh-century. From this survey we can calculate a population of 441 males (or heads of families) for Wirral, which is nearly a quarter of the total for Cheshire as a whole. To arrive at a more accurate figure - if that is possible - we must multiply this total by four or five, in order to include women and children. [43]

Of the 51 manors enumerated for Wirral, (including Guilden Sutton, Wervin, Picton and Mickle Trafford), the largest was Eastham with 85 people and valued at 22 hides. Next came Upton-in-Overchurch with 31 people and 4½ hides. The amount of land valued in Wirral was 97½ hides or 18% of the total for the county.

The Black Death of 1349 may have halved the national population but its local significance for Wirral has not been fully worked out. In 1349 there were several institutions to vacant benefices. Backford, Stoak, Bebington and Woodchurch lacked a priest, Birkenhead a prior. On a wider basis, at least 21 of Cheshire's tenants-in-chief died between the summer and autumn of 1349. [44] If Wirral follows the national pattern it is likely that population was declining before the onset of the bubonic plague, as a result of severe climatic and famine conditions in the early fourteenth-century. [45]

The next complete 'census' for Wirral is the Subsidy Roll of 1545 which contains a total of 700 names. [46] We must bear in mind, however, that early population statistics are frequently unreliable. As Professor Coleman has pointed out, tax returns, military and ecclesiastical records do not take into account 'a familiar lack of enthusiasm for paying taxes, serving in armies or revealing orthodox religious beliefs.' [47]

The county records of the mediaeval period throw considerable light upon the life of the local community. Cheshire had a reputation for disorder and violent crime, and it is clear that Wirral was no exception. [48] Men went out armed, looted in neighbouring counties and killed both man and beast. This lawlessness was no doubt due in part to weak administration by negligent officials who themselves terrorised the populace.

The gentry tended to herd together for criminal activities. In the trailbaston court of 1353, John Domville of Brimstage and Richard Hough of Thornton were accused of illegally hunting in the forest and of leading criminal raids across the Mersey. In reply to this the two men claimed that the Earl of Chester had pardoned them for all burglaries, prison-breaking, rapes, poisonings and conspiracies after the alleged crimes had taken place. [49]

As a result of Cheshire's 'Magna Carta' - confirmed between 1251 and 1389 - a Cheshire subject could be brought to justice only in Cheshire courts, irrespective of where the crime was committed. Henry IV abolished this in 1400.

It seems that even the Wirral Mafia - to use Paul Booth's phrase - were not exempt from violence and vile behaviour. On 23 August 1414 William Stanley was crossing the ferry at Woodside and was assaulted by a band of at least 200 men headed by Sir Henry Norreys of Speke and Richard Bold of Bold.[50]

Until the mid-nineteenth century Wirral was almost exclusively an agricultural area. It is not surprising that the majority of Wirral villages were established on sandstone ridges; the sands and clay around them provided good soil for arable cultivation. [51]

The clergy were particularly active in farming. In the late thirteenth-century the Abbot of Chester was allowed to dig land in Poulton-Lancelyn and Bebington and make ditches to drain the water from Bromborough Mill. [52] He also made marlpits in his manors of Eastham, Irby and Bromborough. These pits were dug to improve the land and the use of boulder clay stiffened the lighter soils.

In the early Middle Ages, the manor was the main economic unit. One half was farmed by the direct management of the lord, or leased out to tenants, the other was composed of holdings let out on lease. The tenants sometimes provided labour for the lord's demesne and had to supply a certain amount of produce from the land. [53]

It is sometimes said that in Wirral this manorial system was never fully developed, but restricted by a large number of small nucleated villages. The fully developed field system was, though, typical of north-west England.[54]

With the growth of population (and therefore increased pressure on the land) and trade in the later Middle Ages, the manor's economic function was superceded by the market. The importance of the market town as a centre for the buying and selling of goods, accounts largely for the rise to prominence of a handful of places in Wirral in the late mediaeval period.

A market was established at Bromborough in 1278 and Burton in 1299. Neston's market status was possibly confirmed by a charter of 1728. [55] The gradual shift of shipping activities on the Dee to places further down the estuary also accounts for the rise in importance of Neston, which became the most populous portion of Wirral in the seventeenth and eighteenth centuries. [56]

The decline of Chester as a port and the growth of Liverpool contributed to a rapid expansion of population on the eastern side of the peninsula. The 1801 census returns showed a total population for Wirral of 10,744. Eighty years later this total was 49,494. [57]

Of the early 'industries' in the district, Domesday mentions several fisheries; at Stanney, Leighton, Gayton, Saughall Massie and Blacon. The same record lists water-mills at Eastham and Prenton. To these we might add Shotwick and Barnston. Mediaeval wind-mills stood at Burton, Bidston, Willaston, Irby, Saughall Massie and Grange. [58]

The early mill structures were of timber and known as peg or post mills. They differed from the later tower mills in that the whole structure moved in the direction of the wind. Only the top part of the tower mill (or cap), with the sails and windshaft, turned to face the wind. [59]

Gayton Mill, just off the main road near the Devon Doorway Restaurant, is an important example of a tower construction of a style dating from the second half of the seventeenth-century. The mill was restored in 1992 for residential use.

6.
Gayton Mill.

29

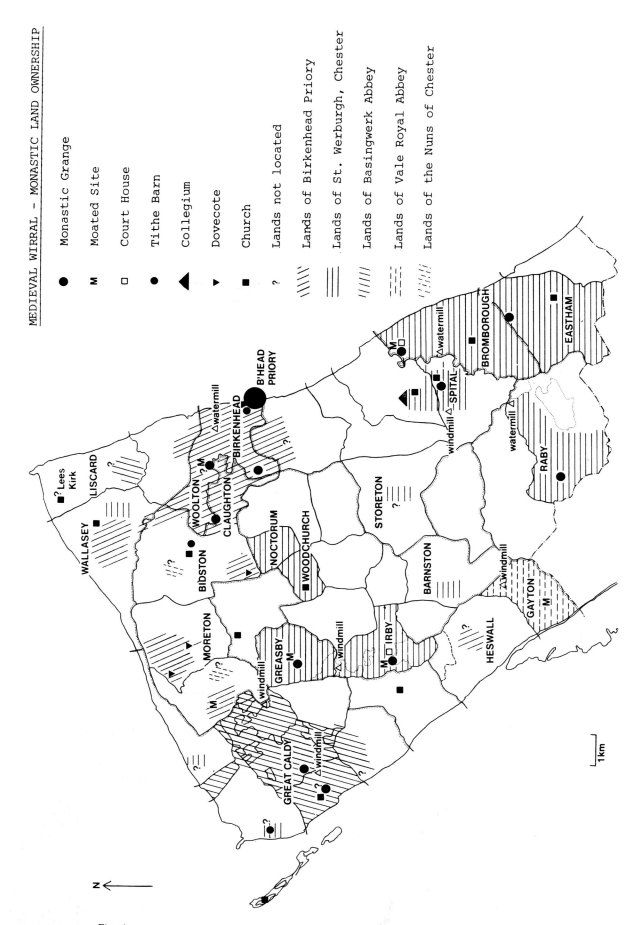

MEDIEVAL WIRRAL – MONASTIC LAND OWNERSHIP

Monastic Grange ●
Moated Site M
Court House □
Tithe Barn ●
Collegium ◄
Dovecote ▶
Church ■
Lands not located ?
Lands of Birkenhead Priory
Lands of St. Werburgh, Chester
Lands of Basingwerk Abbey
Lands of Vale Royal Abbey
Lands of the Nuns of Chester

Fig. 4.
Monastic land ownership in North Wirral from G.Chitty, 'Wirral Rural Fringes Survey Report', Journal of the Merseyside Archaeological Society, *Vol.2, (Liverpool, 1978, reprint 1980).*

(v) THE CHURCH AND THE COMMUNITY

I: The Early Church

The Church to a large extent ordered the tenor of mediaeval life. It was a religious centre, a source of charity and a news service, and it determined the holidays and moral framework of society. The Church also arranged baptisms, burials and weddings.

By the fourth–century, church life in Britain was already complex and established. Christianity would have reached Cheshire in the wake of the Roman legions. One tradition states that St. Germanus of Auxerre visited the Chester district in 429 in order to counter the Pelagian heresy (the idea of obtaining salvation through good works).

The conversion of Wirral to Christianity has been attributed to the missionary work of St. Kentigern in the late sixth–century.[60] Place-name evidence, and that of church dedications, is more conclusive. Celtic churches were probably established at Wallasey and Landican (Woodchurch).[61] Archaeological remains also indicate early Christianity; in particular, the Overchurch stone (Upton) and the cross-fragments from Hilbre, Neston, West Kirby and Bromborough. Early grave-slabs have been found at Overchurch, Woodchurch and Bidston (Church Farm) and at Bebington and Meols.[62]

7.
Pre-Norman cross fragments (Charles Dawson Brown Museum, West Kirby).

The Domesday record gives only four priests for Wirral, at Eastham (Bromborough), Landican (Woodchurch), Neston and Poulton-Lancelyn (Bebington). If we accept the scribe's misorientation, we might add Burton to this list.

The main impact of the Normans in religion was to encourage monasticism. Monastic life had broken down almost completely with the arrival of the Vikings, and the Normans' arrival in England coincided with a monastic revival and expansion in Europe. By 1154 there were nearly 300 monastries in England and well over 5,000 monks.

II: The Abbey of St. Werburgh and the Religious Houses

In 1092 Hugh Lupus, first Earl of Chester, transformed a church of secular canons in Chester into a Benedictine monastery. St. Werburgh's (dedicated to the daughter of a King of Mercia) had probably been founded in the ninth–century by Aethelflaed, the 'Lady of the Mercians.' However, there is no definite evidence for the existence of a church of secular canons at Chester before 958, when King Edgar granted a new charter to St. Werburgh's collegiate church.[63]

The main element in Benedictine monasticism was the practice of humility, and obedience to God, the Rule of St. Benedict and the abbot. The rule was practical in that it advocated labour in the fields and, by implication, economic self-sufficiency as part of the monks' daily routine.

Monasteries were frequently founded by barons as a sort of insurance policy, to enable them to salve their conscience and secure their salvation. The monastery also served an important social function, providing an outlet for noble children in an age of restricted job opportunities.[64]

Benedictine monasticism declined, partly as a result of the rise in prestige of pope and monarchy and partly because it relied too heavily on secular patronage. The Cistercians, on the other hand, came up with a stricter form of the Rule.

They preached a removal from worldly matters and, correspondingly, their buildings were placed in remote spots. In this respect Stanlow Abbey was appropriately situated.

In 1086 the Abbey of St. Werburgh held Croughton, Backford, Little Sutton, Great Saughall, Shotwick, Neston and Raby.[65] By the twelfth-century, the Abbot was the second largest landowner in the county (after the Earl) and controlled a large part of Wirral. Manor houses were established at Little Sutton, Bromborough, Eastham and Irby.

Most of the mediaeval water-mills and wind-mills in Wirral were owned by this religious house. Perhaps most significantly, the abbots were given certain rights and privileges within the forest of Wirral. They could hunt stags and other wild beasts throughout the peninsula and they were relieved of the burden of puture and the sergeants of the peace.[66]

Sometimes a parish church was granted to a monastery. The Abbot usually had the *advowson*, or right to appoint incumbents, and if the church was appropriated to the abbey he also took the church tithes and church property. The monastic appropriator — as rector — had to supply a priest and pay his wages. This priest was the rector's substitute and was known as a *vicar*.

The churches at Wallasey, Bidston, West Kirby and Neston were all attached to Chester Abbey in this fashion. Only Woodchurch and Heswall were independent of monastic influence.

The religious houses in Wirral were founded in the twelfth-century but were never of more than local importance. Birkenhead Priory was apparently independent of Chester Abbey and was founded c.1150 while Stanlow (c.1178) later removed to Whalley in Lancashire.

Two charitable institutions were established in the twelfth-century. There was a house for lepers at Bebington and a hospital for aged and shipwrecked mariners at Denhall, in Burton parish. A leper hospital may also have existed on the boundary of Irby and Thurstaston.[67]

8.
Chapel site, Denhall.

III: The Dissolution and the new Diocese

In 1527 Henry VIII's decision to divorce his first wife sent the government on a course of action known historically as the English Reformation.[68] In 1533 it was stated that the ruler of England was now the supreme authority in both temporal *and* spiritual matters. Finally, in 1534, Henry was accorded the title Supreme Head of the Church in England. The power of the pope had effectively been undermined.

The reasons for this Tudor revolution have been much debated. It is not merely that the king failed to get an annulment of his marriage to Catherine of Aragon, although we certainly cannot rule out his lust for Anne Boleyn and his need for a male heir. In the early sixteenth-century, the church was riddled with corruption. A flood of anti-clerical pamphlets flowed from the newly invented printing press, and preachers drew attention to the problem of clergy who grew wealthy, failed to appear in church and who harboured concubines.

On a local level, people objected to the tithes, fees and levies extracted by the parish church. On a wider level, Cardinal Wolsey epitomised the wealth and worldliness with which the English Church had become associated. Not surprisingly his downfall came on the eve of the dramatic religious changes wrought by Henry VIII and his minister Thomas Cromwell.

The fact that the government achieved these sweeping changes without much opposition indicates a certain lack of enthusiasm and distaste for clericalism. The changes were supported by the politically conscious and active classes, and it was these people who stood to gain most from the crown's takeover of church property.

The monasteries were the tangible remnants of a now redundant religiosity and it was inevitable that they, and the churches, would fall under the government's gaze. Most important, Henry VIII needed money and the religious buildings were an important source of revenue. The relics, images, furnishings — even the lead from the roofs — were plundered for the crown's coffers. A list of ornaments, drawn up 1549-50, shows the paucity of possessions in Wirral churches.[69]

A commission was set up to inquire into the property and revenue of the religious establishments. The outcome was a detailed assessment of all clerical income, the *Valor Ecclesiasticus* of 1535. Professor Dickens has called this 'the most informative single source on the economic history of the Tudor Church, and is worthy in its fashion to be placed alongside Domesday Book.'[70] Birkenhead Priory was valued at £102 16s. 9½d.[71]

In 1536 the lesser monastic houses, including Birkenhead, surrendered their lands. The dispossessed monks were pensioned off; some would no doubt have transferred to neighbouring churches. The heads of houses received a better pension than their surbordinates and in many cases they rose to bishoprics and deaneries.

The Dissolution involved the transfer of vast amounts of land to new owners, although many ecclesiastical properties had passed into lay hands before 1536. These new owners were the rising gentry who were beginning to make themselves heard in parliament by the end of the century. In Wirral those who gained from crown grants of land included the Gleggs, Stanleys and Pooles.

From the eleventh-century Cheshire was part of the diocese of Coventry and Lichfield. The 'new' diocese of Chester was founded in August 1541, but its size made the administration of the Church a formidable task. The diocese included the whole of Lancashire and Cheshire, parts of Flintshire, Cumberland and Westmorland, and a large area of Yorkshire.[72]

IV: Reformation and Recusancy in Wirral

The establishment of Henrician Catholicism, or Catholicism without a pope, and later, Elizabethan Anglicanism, did not lead to a sudden conformity amongst clergy or laity. In the late sixteenth-century there is strong evidence that sermons were missed, prescribed texts were not available, few clergy were graduates and many incumbents were absentees.[73] Geoffrey Blythe, for example, was rector of West Kirby from 1526-1541. He was also Master of the King's Hall, Cambridge and officiated at Lichfield. He possibly never set foot in West Kirby.[74]

In February 1568 Queen Elizabeth I wrote to the Bishop of Chester, William Downham, and informed him that his diocese was lacking in discipline.[75]

Elizabeth's government knew that here was a potential hotbed of Catholic recusancy, and fears were increased after the queen's excommunication in 1572 and the threat of Spanish invasion in the 1580s. In 1586 there was 'a sudden and fearefull hew and crye...that there was a navye of 700 Spanyardes shipps landed at New Key in Worrall...But the crye was false and proved contrary.'[76]

Among those Wirral families with Catholic sympathies were the Masseys of Puddington, the Whitmores of Thurstaston, the Stanleys of Hooton, the Houghs of Leighton and the Hockenhalls of Prenton. However most English Catholics were also good anglophiles. Rowland Stanley of Hooton, for example, was embarassed by his son William's decision to defect to the Catholic side whilst in the Netherlands. He gave £100 to the Armada fund.[77] In 1587 the queen appealed for horses and weapons. It is noticeable that most of the Catholic families in Wirral gave generously.[78]

As K.R. Wark has pointed out, in an article of 1971, the imprisonment of men like John Whitmore and John Hockenhall may have limited the spread of religious dissidence in Wirral.[79]

While it can be argued that the Elizabethan religious settlement achieved unity for the English people, its effective enforcement depended largely upon the efficiency of administration and the quality of personnel. It was claimed in the 1580's that 'the bishop (of Chester) frequents those (parsonages) infected with popery, on pretext of seeking their reformation, but never yet reformed any.'[80]

The bishop's visitation aimed to discover church abuses, the condition of church fabric and ornaments, the conduct of services, and absenteeism and adultery.[81] More frequently, these enquiries into lay and clerical behaviour were more intent on making profit, than making reform.

The visitation records give us some insight into the plight of the clergy — poorly paid and badly educated — and the indifference of the local community. Much popular religion probably had little to do with Christianity at all. The Elizabethan reforms deprived people of those superstitious customs and rituals which proved comforting. People may have turned to magic, mysticism, and even witchcraft.[82]

At Woodchurch, in 1592, the churchwardens were accused of slackness. They had failed to fine absentees 1s. a week for not coming to church. One parishioner had been married in her father's house, rather than in church.[83]

It was claimed that the farmers of Bidston 'have had noe sermons but one bie a stranger.' At Bromborough the church was 'verie ruinous in so much they are not able to saie service and there books and Register bee spoiled and they require reformation.'[84]

The curate at Heswall failed to catechise and make collections. At Eastham 'They wante the second tome of Homilus; they have not levied xii d. of the absents; they want collectores.'[85] At the visitation of 1605 the vicar at Eastham had no ecclesiastical garb and William Whitmore of Leighton and his wife Alice were accused of non-attendance for the past twelve months.[86]

In 1619 it was reported that ale was being sold at West Kirby rectory and, in 1625, the curate at Bromborough was thought to be a drunkard.[87] By the 1630's the religious situation may have been changing. Clerical standards had improved and most clergy were now graduates. In 1625 the Earl of Derby reported to the government that Cheshire 'had very few recusants and those not dangerous.'[88]

A real transformation was not effected until 1629 when King James I issued instructions to bishops, aimed at tightening up their administration. In 1632 the king described Chester as one of those sees where 'the revenues have been so diminished that they suffice not to maintain the bishop.' Meagre remuneration accounts for many of the problems during the sixteenth–century. The Church failed to attract educated and qualified people because of the poor wages. Bishop Chadderton (who succeeded Downham in 1579) described his incumbents as 'very beggarly vicars and curates.'

(vi) THE WIRRAL GENTRY

During the Middle Ages life in Wirral was dominated by a small group of leading families some of whom played an active role in war.[89] Fighting was a traditional occupation, and there was the popular conception that society was divided into those who toiled, those who prayed, and those who fought. The man of noble breeding found in war the opportunity for personal or collective glory and an escape from the humdrum routine of life. More especially, war meant booty, and success brought royal favour; land, offices, prestige.

In the later Middle Ages, large numbers of Cheshire knights and serving men were drafted into the Hundred Years War with France. The Cheshire archers are, of course, famous in military history and formed the backbone of Richard II's government. When Richard II mounted an expedition to Ireland, his personal bodyguard was recruited from Cheshire by Sir John Stanley of Hooton. Later, William Stanley and Sir John Massey were among the Cheshire captains.

Warfare was merely one aspect of life for the Wirral gentry, although a significant one, and they were also local administrators, tax collectors, justices and police. Competition for offices was keen.[90]

The Stanley family had a grip on the office of sheriff and chamberlain in the late fifteenth-century. Sir William Stanley was made sheriff for life in February 1466 and the Stanleys held the chamberlainship continuously from 1461 to 1494. William Stanley was also Constable of Flint and Rhuddlan Castle.

The Stanleys of Hooton and Storeton were the senior branch of this old Staffordshire family, and the ancestors of the Earl of Derby. They held the manor of Storeton and the bailiwick of Wirral forest from 1310 and the manor of Hooton by 1411. In 1405 Sir John Stanley, son of the third Sir William Stanley, and son-in-law of Sir Thomas Lathom, received a grant of the Isle of Man. The lordship remained with the Stanley family until 1736.[91]

Some of the duties of the Stanley family included raising troops and running errands for the king. On the battle-field at Bosworth, they played an important part in turning events in favour of Henry Tudor.

The Massey family held Puddington from the time of the Conquest until 1715. The family's chief seat was at Dunham Massey, near Altrincham. Representatives of this house were prominent in the king's military forces. Sir William Massey of Puddington was killed at the Battle of Shrewsbury in 1403; Masseys also aided Charles I, and the last of the line — another William Massey and a devoted Catholic — took part in the Jacobite rising of 1715. Subsequently Puddington passed to the Stanleys of Hooton, who assumed the name Massey-Stanley.

The Troutbecks, who originated in Westmorland, held land in Brimstage, Woodchurch and Little Neston. Their fortune was closely tied up with royal favour as a result of military action.

In 1412 William Troutbeck (d.1444) was made chamberlain of Chester by Henry, Prince of Wales, and he held this office until 1439. From 1423 until 1439 he was also chancellor of the Duchy of Lancaster.

His son, John (d.1458) extended the family estates partly as a result of marrying Margery Hulse. He acquired a further portion of Little Neston and during this period Brimstage was obtained.

The Troutbecks were actively involved in military campaigns. The eldest son of John Troutbeck was killed at Bloreheath in September 1459 fighting for Lancashire. (This was the first important engagement in which the Cheshire gentry took part). His youngest son, William, fought at Bosworth against the Yorkists. In 1487 he helped Henry VII defeat Lambert Simnel's followers at the Battle of Stoke.

William died in 1510 and as there were no direct heirs the Troutbeck estates passed by marriage to John Talbot, ancestor of the earls of Shrewsbury.[92]

The Whitmores of Thurstaston possessed this manor from the late thirteenth century until 1715, and claimed descent from Ranulf, third Earl of Chester. The family remained attached to the old faith at the Reformation and the transcript of the parish register for Thurstaston(1581) records the recusancy of two members of the Whitmore family and their wives.[93]

(vii) WIRRAL'S ARCHITECTURAL HERITAGE

I: Vernacular Buildings

In his book *The History of the Hundred of Wirral* (1847), William Williams Mortimer wrote that 'Few good specimens of ancient architecture remain in Wirral.'[94] Admittedly, there is nothing on the scale of Little Moreton Hall and there is no great castle, but the old buildings of Wirral are scarcely less interesting for this.

Wirral abounds in examples of what has been termed *vernacular architecture*; the 'lesser' houses and cottages as opposed to the great manor houses. Of the four generally accepted size-types, Wirral has no great houses, some 'large' houses, and many 'small' houses and cottages.

The size of the house is commensurate with the wealth of the owner. Indeed, this is why houses make such a fascinating study. The plan, arrangement of the rooms, the furnishings and fittings, and the method of construction, can tell us much about the owners and tenants through the ages. The value of building study has only recently been acknowledged as an important contribution to social and economic history.[95]

For centuries, farm-workers and their families lived in hovels — crude 'shelters' built to keep out the weather but not built to survive. Simple cottages, like Pear Tree in Raby and the building behind Rock Villa in West Kirby, give us some indication of early artisan housing. Although these examples are actually quite late, the style of building probably changed little through the centuries.

9.
Cottage at Rock Villa, West Kirby.

In early times builders used local sources of supply — material that was easily transported to the site. The abundancy of the keuper sandstone in Wirral provided the raw material for most of the peninsula's buildings. Consequently, the Wirral landscape is characterised by soft reddish-brown stone.

10.
Old House at Greasby (corner of Mill Lane and Greasby Road). Courtesy Liverpool City Library.

The supply of timber would have been readily available in mediaeval Wirral, and we can assume that timber-framed buildings were once widespread in the district. The inner courtyard at Puddington Old Hall preserves a fine example of timber framing, dating from the late fifteenth-century. Some decidedly 'modern' looking buildings, such as Poulton and Gayton Hall, have early origins. The roughcast and brick exterior betrays a wooden framed internal structure.

Among the earliest structural systems was that of the *cruck* frame, when a pair of inclined timbers were set as a gable end. At Vineyard Farm, Poulton-Lancelyn, there is Wirral's finest cruck-framed structure, an early seventeenth-century barn.[96] On the south-side of Village Street, Burton, the much-altered Delamere House incorporates fourteenth-century crucks at first floor level. A cruck-framed out building existed until 1965 at 'Bird's House', Poulton, Wallasey.[97]

11.
Cruck-built barn (Vineyard Farm, Poulton-Lancelyn).

The alternative building system was that of the box frame, in which pairs of posts supported cross beams. Local examples include Poulton Hall, Old Red Lion and Ash Tree Farm (both in Willaston). The walling of these houses originally consisted of wattle and daub, a mixture of mud, cattle droppings, hazel and brushwood staves, which provided the mediaeval builder with infill material.

C2.

By the late Middle Ages, lead began to replace shingle (oak tiles) and thatch as a roofing material. Thatch, consisting of reed, straw and heather, was particularly useful because it had insulating properties. By its nature, however, this material is perishable and no original thatch roofing survives in Wirral. Fine examples of the seventeenth-century single-storeyed thatched cottage exist at Lower Bebington (25 The Village) and 'Barn End' (Rock Cottage) on the north side of Village Street, Burton.

12.
Barn End, Burton.

13.
Old roof trusses, Shotwick Lodge Farm.

14.
The old house ('Bird's Tenement'), Wallasey.

The most common form of roof construction in the thirteenth-century was the *tie-beam*. The main rafters - or principals - were given extra support by a central *king-post*. The finest example of this type, in Wirral, is preserved at Pensby Hall. Old roof trusses are also preserved in the north wing of a farm outbuilding at Shotwick Lodge Farm.

During the early fourteenth-century, the tie-beam roof fell out of favour and was increasingly replaced by the *arch-braced* construction. The principals were supported by the continously curved arch braces tied together towards the top of the roof by a collar beam. The finest example of this in Wirral, dating from Tudor times, is preserved at Stoak, Church of St. Lawrence.

Brick as a building material had for a long time a sort of snob and status value. It was used in England as early as the thirteenth-century but its use did not become widespread until the late sixteenth-century and, in Cheshire, even later. The Old Hall and the north wing of Ash Tree Farm, in Willaston, and Gayton Hall, afford examples of early brick building.

Of the windows, the characteristic type in Wirral is the mullioned division. Even in the late seventeenth-century glazing may have been unusual in windows of this type. Hinged or sliding shutters may have provided security and draught protection.

Mediaeval doorways were generally frameless. In the seventeenth-century it became common practice to decorate the stone over the doorway with coats of arms, initials, and dates. In Wirral many houses were decorated like this but one has to be careful about using the stones as dating evidence.[98]

These tablets may have been brought in from elsewhere or reset after alterations. Some, such as the modern inscription over the door at Willaston Hall, may recall old furnishings or internal fittings. The datestones in Wirral have been frequently misinterpreted. For example, the stone over the door at 'Bird's House' in Wallasey has been read as 1697 when it looks more like 1621.

The dates inscribed on internal fittings, such as chimney-pieces, are even less reliable. Very frequently these would have been moved from place to place, not necessarily in the same house. Unfortunately, many of the ornamental inscriptions in Wirral have been lost due to constant erosion by the weather. Sandstone is easily worked and shaped, but it is also easily weathered.[99]

Due to the efforts of local conservation groups, Wirral possesses a few examples of early windmills. The mediaeval post-type was light, timber-framed and not durable. The tower mill was made of brick or stone and became widespread in England in the eighteenth-century. Examples exist at Gayton, Willaston, Bidston and Saughall.

Finally, in this brief summary of vernacular architecture in Wirral, we might mention the columbarium or dovecote. This is a fascinating survival from the days when pigeons were considered to be a useful source of fresh meat. Seventeenth century dovecotes survive at Gayton and Puddington Old Hall.

Perhaps the most noticeable aspect of Wirral's early architecture is the conservatism, and uniformity of building styles. The mellowed stone farmhouse is typical and repeated across the peninsula. 'Bird's House' (Wallasey), Church Farm (Bidston), Stanhope House (Bromborough) and Pensby, Greasby and Oldfield Halls fall into this category.

15.
Pensby Hall.

16.
Oxton Old Hall.

Most of Wirral's early farm buildings have undergone continuous alteration and adaption by successive generations. While this has preserved the structure in some form or another, it has often changed it beyond recognition. Windows are blocked up, mullions broken and interesting architectural features lost under whitewash.

A general revival in building in late sixteenth, and early seventeenth century England was noticed by Professor Hoskins.[100] The Elizabethan chronicler, William Harrison, described this as the 'great amendment of lodging', the visual demonstration of social standing - of a populace trying to better themselves and their neighbours. Money for building schemes came from land, from agriculture, and from the profits of war and administration.

The 'great rebuilding' is reflected in the manor houses of Wirral, often with a subsequent history of alterations and additions. Bidston Hall is a particularly fine example of this house type; others exist at Poulton, Gayton, Thurstaston and Brimstage, where part of the fourteenth-century manor house and its fortified tower still stand adjoined to the later (post mediaeval) hall.

II: Church Buildings

The parish church has been likened to an old man's bicycle - the fittings and fabric may change frequently but it still remains basically the same.[101] In mediaeval times the church building dominated the landscape. The fabric is a testimony to the masons, wood carvers, painters and other craftsmen through the ages. It is both a monument of village pride and a museum of community life.

There are no pre-Conquest church buildings extant in Wirral, largely as a result of the ephemeral nature of the building material. Woodchurch, for example, is indicative, Hilbre appears in mediaeval records as Wodecot, and Bebington was once called Whitechurch, possibly to distinguish it from the more usual wood structures.

We have already mentioned that the Domesday Book records a priest for Eastham (Bromborough), Landican (Woodchurch), Neston, Poulton-Lancelyn (Bebington) and Burton. On the basis of archaeological and place-name evidence we might add to this list of eleventh-century churches, Wallasey, Bidston, West Kirby and Shotwick. Religious houses existed at Birkenhead and Stanlow, from the late twelfth-century.

The simple 'three-celled plan' of nave, choir and sanctuary was gradually replaced at this time by a cruciform arrangement. Square, projecting transepts were added (north and south) between the nave and the chancel to form the shape of a cross.

It is widely assumed that this plan represented the Cross of Christ, and the slight misalignment between chancel and nave has been taken as a reference to the droop of Christ's head on the Cross. However, the misalignment is also found in churches which are *not* cruciform in plan and it probably results from the separate rebuilding of church and nave. The 'weeping' chancel is a feature of Holy Cross, Woodchurch.

Of Norman architecture still *in situ* we have in Wirral the chapter house at Birkenhead Priory, carefully restored and re-opened in 1919, a decorated doorway at Shotwick, and capitals (head or top part of a column) at Bebington, West Kirby and Neston.

17.
Norman capital (Church of St. Andrew, Bebington).

Four twelfth-century churches have disappeared; Overchurch (demolished 1813) occupied a site near the present motorway interchange on Upton Road, Moreton, and only an overgrown grave-yard exists. Thurstaston (1824), Stoak (1827) and Bromborough (1828) have all been rebuilt.

At Bidston and Wallasey only the tower remains from the late mediaeval period. Both are similar in construction to those at Shotwick and Backford, and reflect what Fred Crossley (a leading authority on church architecture) described as 'The real age of tower building in Cheshire,' which began towards the close of the fifteenth-century.[102]

Tower building was part of a general revival in church rebuilding and refurbishing at this time. Elaborate building schemes were set afoot after the horrors of the Black Death and the War of the Roses, when money was simply not available, and resulted from the wider distribution of wealth and continuing trade expansion. There was the construction of aisles and roofs and, in order to create an undivided chancel, the chancel arch was removed in what has been called the 'West Cheshire' style.[103]

During this period there was also an increased enthusiasm for glass to add a sense of spaciousness and light. Fragments of early glass survive at Woodchurch, Eastham and Shotwick.

The late fourteenth-century saw the final phase of Gothic architecture — the Perpendicular — when curves and convolutions gave way to the use of straight lines. The Perpendicular arches in the chancel at Bebington suggest a grandeur quite unique in local church building. If the Bebington building scheme had survived the Dissolution, the church would have rated with the finest of Cheshire.[104] As it stands, it vies with Shotwick as the finest old Wirral church.

18.
Church tower, Backford (Church of St. Oswald).

With the Dissolution, and the review of clerical incomes, came vandalism, destruction and plundering, which continued unabated until the time of the Restoration. Church visitation records and, in particular, the churchwarden accounts, tell of the decline of church fabric and fittings.[105] At Woodchurch and Wallasey, in 1634, there were faulty seats while at Shotwick and Bebington the chancel was in need of repair.

19.
Tudor arches (Church of St. Andrew, Bebington).

Many pieces of church furniture were lost during the Reformation and the Civil War. The religious changes of Edward VI's and Elizabeth I's reign meant that various fittings disappeared. For example, the parson had to be seen as well as heard, so the rood screen was removed.

Parish chests survive to a great extent, and fonts are very indicative of an early church where other evidence fails.[106] Old bells survive at Stoak and Shotwick and late mediaeval woodwork exists at Woodchurch.[107]

Chapter II

Wallasey and North Wirral

(i) WALLASEY

Topographically, Wallasey is almost an island and must have appeared so to the early settlers. It is bounded on the north by the Irish Sea, on the east by the Mersey, and to the south and south-east by the River Birket which widens into Wallasey Pool. Wallasey's isolated position at the far north of Wirral -surrounded by water and marshland - has affected its historical development.

Wallasey is not really a town at all but a collection of villages and hamlets; Poulton-cum-Seacombe, Liscard, and Kirkby in Walley. The last named was the original settlement and it literally means the church village in the island of Welshmen. The district may have been a refuge for Romanised Britons sheltering from the English invaders and there is evidence to suggest an unbroken Christian tradition from the fifth-century.[1]

In the Domesday survey of 1086, Robert de Rodelent (Rhuddlan) held the lands of 'Walea' from his uncle Hugh Lupus, the first Earl of Chester. After Robert's death, the lands were carved up amongst a large number of freeholders or yeoman. The rather fragmented manors in Wallasey probably contributed to the piecemeal development of the area from about 1880 onwards.

The Becheton or Bechinton family and the Litherlands held important manorial property here in the Middle Ages and, until 1609, Liscard was held by the Astons. After this time the estates passed to the Meols family.

In the seventeenth-century Wallasey achieved fame throughout the country for its race-course, possibly the first of its kind in England.[2] In 1735 the course extended from a point near the junction of the present Green Lane and Wallasey Village and stretched almost to Leasowe Castle. Close to the starting and finishing post, on a site now occupied by part of Sandiways Road, stood the stables which were later known as Sandfield Hall.

In 1897 we know that 'of the stables, some ruinous buildings still remain among trees in a field off the road that runs through the village going eastward at Wallasey. One gateway is much after the design of that at old Bidston Hall.'[3] The following year the ruins were destroyed 'to make way for several rows of brick and mortar abominations.'[4] An old door from the racing stable was later removed to Liverpool Museum but was unfortunately destroyed as a result of the fire in 1941.

20.
The old house ('Bird's Tenement'), Wallasey.

One has to look hard to find physical evidence of Wallasey's past. Much of it has been bulldozed to oblivion. One old building is now dwarfed by the menacing tanks of the United Molasses Company, at the corner of Limekiln Lane and Poulton Bridge Road. 'The Old House' or 'Bird's Tenement' has a 1621 datestone but was probably built in the second half of the seventeenth-century. It is an excellent example of a yeoman farmer's dwelling and was thought worthy of preservation by the old Wallasey Borough Council.

It is a shame that the same could not be said for Mother Redcap's. This old house, much altered through the centuries, was late sixteenth-century in origin and occupied a site between the present Caithness and Lincoln Drives. It took its name from the owner, in the days when the building was an integral part of the local smuggling trade.[5] In 1973 the house was described as 'a massive mess on the seafront' - a monument of rot and graffiti. However, as journalist Ian Roth passionately pointed out:

> 'What does it matter how much of the genuine
> (sixteenth) century fabric remains? Whatever might
> have gone, how many may have been the changes, the
> romance is still there, the legends - of smugglers, of
> buried gold - linger on...It is one of the last
> remaining links with Wallasey's past.'[6]

This last remaining link was severed in October 1974. After ill-fated attempts to incorporate Mother Redcap's in the North Wirral Coastal Park, and even an idea to remove the structure - physically - to Bidston, the bulldozer moved in. At the time of writing, the site remains undeveloped.

21.
Mother Redcap's. Courtesy Wallasey Reference Library Collection.

LEASOWE CASTLE

Leasowe Castle is an architectural pot-pourri, but what it lacks in aesthetic value it makes up for in character and tradition. The place breathes history.

The basic octagonal structure is thought to date from the late sixteenth-century, and this original tower may have been built for Ferdinando, fifth Earl of Derby. He was the grandson of Mary, eldest daughter of Henry VII, and a likely claimant to the English throne. The present Princess of Wales is actually related to Ferdinando: in 1579 he married Alice, daughter of Sir John Spencer of Althorp.

It is not really clear why the original tower was built. The old theory that the site was a good vantage point for the horse racing on the Leasowes is not really tenable as the start and finish of the race was two miles away.[7] The thickness of the walls may indicate that this was no mere aristocratic whim, but a fortification and place of refuge. There is also the suggestion that the building was ideally situated as a stopping off place for the Isle of Man and Ireland. (The earls of Derby were kings of Man from the fifteenth-century).

Four square towers were built on to alternate faces of the original structure and this accounts for the 1593 datestone - thought to have been over the original doorway - appearing on an inside wall.[8] The two remaining turrets may have been added some time in the early seventeenth-century as they closely resemble the architectural style of the racing stable which, until 1898, stood at the top of Sandiways Road in Wallasey.[9]

The door jambs of the original entrance can still be seen, eight to nine feet above floor level, near the old dining room. It seems likely that some sort of staircase was used to gain entry.

In the early seventeenth-century the building was known as New Hall, possibly to distinguish it from Wallasey Hall which was built about 1600. It may have been used as a sporting residence for the earls of Derby, housing visiting hawkers and horsemen. The nearby Leasowe race-course was described as 'one of the finest grounds of its length in England' and attracted riders from all over the country.[10]

By the end of the century, the building was clearly in a state of dilapidation; it appears in records and maps as Mockbeggar Hall, a traditional name applied to tumbledown residences. This decline was no doubt hastened by the wavering fortunes of the earls of Derby whose land was confiscated as a result of the Civil War.

The name 'Leasowe Castle' first appears in the bill of sale when the property passed in 1802 to the widow of Lewis W. Boode.[11] Mrs. Boode made considerable alterations and additions in 1818, and during her ownership the house frequently received the survivors of the many shipwrecks off the North Wirral coast.

Mrs. Boode's daughter married Colonel Edward Cust in January 1821, to whom the building passed on the death of his mother-in-law. Cust was an important military figure, a historian and collector, and in 1847 became Master of Ceremonies to Queen Victoria.

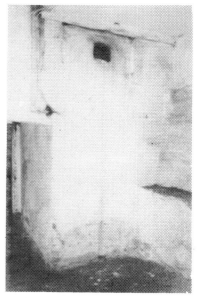

22.
Door jambs, Leasowe Castle.

He was responsible for many additions and alterations to the Castle; he probably added the surrounding wall, the gates and gate-house, the so-called Canute's Chair, and the legend of the mermaid.

The dining room on the ground floor (now the 'Star Chamber Bar') was decorated with oak panelling from the Star Chamber at Westminster, purchased when the old Exchequer buildings were demolished in 1836. (The Star Chamber was a judicial court dating from the fifteenth-century). Sadly, these panels were removed, along with the furnishings, in 1893.[12]

The room once known as the Board Room, now on a mezzanine level, was fitted out with bog oak from the submerged forest at Meols. Again, this oak has been removed.

After Cust's death in 1878, the Castle passed to his only son. Then, in 1893, the building and grounds were offered for sale and all fittings and furniture were disposed of. Finally, the property was bought by the Trustees of the Railwaymen's Convalescent Homes and after alterations was reopened in June 1911. It was used as a rest home until 1970, apart from a spell of military use during the first world war when it became a prisoner-of-war camp.

Leasowe Castle was bought by Wallasey Borough Council in April 1974 for £113,000, shortly before county reorganisation. It became the proverbial 'white elephant.' The new Wirral Borough Council remained undecided and divided about its future and were not prepared to authorise repairs. Leasowe Castle became a repository for council rubbish, and the fabric began to deteriorate.

In August 1979 the Castle was again up for sale, and it was suggested that it be used for leisure, recreation or entertainment purposes 'in sympathy with the council's general concept of the recreational role of the North Wirral coastal area.'[13] Plans to make the building into a youth hostel had previously been thrown out.

In July 1980 a local businessman came forward with an idea to turn the Castle and grounds into a conference centre, hotel and caravan park. Local conservationists opposed the plan as they thought that caravans would spoil the landscape. Wirral's planning committee gave their approval in September 1980 and the Castle reopened in December 1982 in its new role as leisure centre.

The present owner should be applauded for his enterprise, but the council should have restored and revived the Castle as a place of historic interest and made it the focal point of the coastal park. It might have become a local arts and crafts-cum-history museum or a study centre for local schoolchildren designed to make them more aware of local history and heritage.

23.
Leasowe Castle, from the south-east.

CHURCH OF ST. HILARY AND THE OLD RECTORY

The dedication to St. Hilary is unusual in that it is only one of seven in the country. The others are largely scattered around Cornwall and Wales. This Celtic connection is strengthened by the place-name Kirkby in Walley and the suggestion that a circular churchyard may have once existed here.[14]

Archaeologically, there has been no trace of a Celtic or Saxon church although in the nineteenth-century a deep bed of mussel shells was discovered near the site. This indicated a possible sub-Roman camp and it is tempting to conclude that this may have been the very place of refuge for the Romanised Britons. The site occupies a very commanding position and could have been used for defensive purposes in earlier times.

24.
Site of Church of St. Hilary, Wallasey, from the south.

In the nineteenth-century fragments of Norman masonry were discovered, including a font, arch-stone and part of a chancel arch. We know that c.1162-82 William de Walley required a burial place in the chancel.[15] The font, which apparently lay in the north-west corner of the church, was put out in the church garden in the nineteenth–century. It can now be found in St. Luke's, Poulton.[16]

The church of St. Hilary was rebuilt in the thirteenth-and fourteenth- centuries. A fourth church on this site since 1066 was erected in the early sixteenth-century. The present tower, standing to the south of the modern church, is dated 1530 and is all that remains from the late mediaeval period. It was restored in the nineteenth-century for use as a mortuary chapel.

Although the tower is said to contain material from the early Norman structure, the windows, gargoyles and motifs place its construction in the reign of Henry VIII. We know, also, that money was given for the tower in 1527.[17]

A fifth church was built about 1757-60 and was described as barn-like and 'plain even to ugliness.' In the early hours of Sunday February 1 1857 this church was gutted by fire and later that day 'presented nothing but a heap of smouldering ruins.'[18] It is said that the sexton had been over-enthusiastic in stoking the fires in readiness for the morning service. Fortunately, the priceless parish registers (dating back to 1574) and other valuable documents were saved from the flames by the rector.[19]

The existence of another mediaeval church in Wallasey was first suggested by Henry Robinson in 1727.[20] In his *Account of Wallazey* he supplies a fanciful description of the Lees Kirk and the story is repeated by Bishop Gastrell who reported that it stood 'near a narrow Land still called Kirkway.'[21]

The present road of that name, joining Earlston Road and Mount Pleasant Road, was built in 1923 and is supposed to occupy the old site of the church. However, no traces of old buildings were found during construction work. If a church, or chapel, did exist it probably would have served the people of Liscard ('Lees' derived from Ilys, the Celtic name for a court or manor house) or the manor house on the site now occupied by Wallasey Central Library.[22]

Other writers give the location of this mysterious church at Leasowe, near the lighthouse. An ancient burial-ground was supposedly discovered here in the 1820s.[23] The most likely explanation for Robinson's two churches, is that he was confused by the split of the advowson in the years 1174-84. William de Walley gave half the advowson to Birkenhead Priory, and half to the Abbey of St. Werburgh in Chester.[24]

The building to the south of the modern rectory, half way down Church Hill, has for many years fallen victim to vandalism and decay. From the early seventeenth-century until 1936 it was used as the rector's residence and after the second world war it became a meeting-place for parish societies. The building ceased to be used early in 1975, and in July 1976 the local council demanded its restoration. The following year the church authorities wanted the old rectory demolished; it had become an eyesore.

In April 1978 a local man bought the property for £15,500. The building was sold again in the summer of 1981 and the present owners now plan to restore the structure using traditional materials.[25]

The old rectory is thought to date from 1632; during restoration work in 1978 an old fireplace was discovered with the Latin inscription, *Domum Gorg Snell Fieri Fecit.* George Snell was rector at Wallasey church from 1619-35 and probably acquired the rectory from his predecessor, Thomas Fletcher.

Further alterations to the structure were made in 1695 by Thomas Swinton and a tablet, now incorporated in the modern rectory, records (in Latin) that he built the brick part of the house. The Rev. F. Haggitt used some of the stones from Wallasey Old Hall to build the gabled end of the old rectory. (The Old Hall, built c.1600, stood on the site now occupied by the modern rectory and was pulled down in 1862-3).

25.
Norman font, (Church of St. Luke, Poulton).

26.
Old fireplace, Old Rectory.

47

27.
The Old Rectory and church tower, Wallasey.

MORETON AND SAUGHALL MASSIE

Moreton and Saughall Massie were never really part of Wallasey at all.[26] They were originally attached to the parish of Bidston which itself was part of the large manor of Eastham. In mediaeval times, Moreton was the most prosperous of the Bidston townships and in the 1406 tax assessment known as the Mize, Moreton was one of Wirral's largest tax-payers.[27] The Prior of Birkenhead held lands here until 1536, when they were leased to an official of the Diocese of Chester.[28]

Sadly, there is little left in Moreton - 'the village on the marsh' - to illustrate its essentially rural past. The old historical centre, at Barnston Lane, is now lost amongst houses and shops. One old farmhouse remains, dated 1719, which contains an oak beam in an upstairs room which may come from an earlier construction.[29]

Saughall Massie is now a Conservation Area, but the planners and developers have hacked away at its heritage. Several old houses remain and some barns have old stone plinths to the brick walls, a feature found in rebuilt timber structures. The monks of Birkenhead held lands here until the mid sixteenth-century.

28.
Ivy Cottage, Saughall Massie.

(ii) MEOLS AND THE SUBMERGED FOREST

The coastlands and foreshore in North Wirral consist chiefly of a series of 'post-glacial' beds. These peat and forest layers have been found on Bidston Moss and in the bed of Wallasey Pool during construction of the docks, but they are not a phenomenon peculiar to Wirral. Similar submerged layers occur on the Liverpool side of the Mersey estuary, at Seaforth, and Rhyl on the North Wales coast. The sand dunes which cover these beds on the margin of the shore at Meols, (and at one time Wallasey), contain near their base layers of dark soil, which probably represent old land surfaces.[30]

The name Meols (Domesday, *Melas*) may be derived from the Norse term for hills or sand-banks. The name Dove Point - the site of possible prehistoric, Roman mediaeval occupation - may come from the Celtic *dhu* (i.e. black) as applied to the dark coloured peat beds exposed on the shore.

The antiquities discovered on this north shore near Meols belong to many different periods. They were collected by several nineteenth-century antiquaries and over 3,000 items were catalogued in Hume's book, *Ancient Meols*, published in 1863. Liverpool Museum received four groups of Meols material but much was lost as a result of the fire which destroyed the museum in 1941. The Potter and Longueville collections are now at the Grosvenor Museum in Chester and there is other material in Warrington Museum and the Williamson Art Gallery and Museum, Birkenhead.[31]

Hume believed that Meols was a Roman outpost 'not only for the purpose of embarking and disembarking with greater facility in their sea journeys, but as a permanent outwork and place of observation.'[32]

The Roman and British finds are sufficient to suggest some occupation, perhaps a small outpost, and if a Roman site did exist it was quite possibly 'nearly a mile seaward of the present high-water mark of spring tide, and westward of Leasowe Castle.'[33] Roman coins were found east of that part of the shore where mediaeval finds predominated, a site near Leasowe lighthouse.

Although the advancing waters may have driven the coastal settlement in a south-west direction, the quantity of finds seems to indicate a prosperous community suddenly abandoned rather than a gradual drift of population to another site.[34] Dr. G. Lloyd-Morgan of the Grosvenor Museum, Chester, has concluded that the Roman finds from Meols can tell us little about the nature of occupation here but she does note that a couple of the finds are normally found on military sites.[35]

Of the Anglo-Saxon coin finds, there is a noteable absence from the period 900-973 when the newly established Chester Mint was so productive. These coin finds may have been the result of casual loss rather than intense settlement.[36]

The majority of artefacts relate to the thirteenth-century, a possible indication of the height of this settlement's prosperity. The most characteristic finds are small belt-fittings and buckles. Other finds include flints, brooches, pins, beads, knives and bells. Lighter objects, such as pottery, were probably carried out below low tide mark and so not recovered.[37]

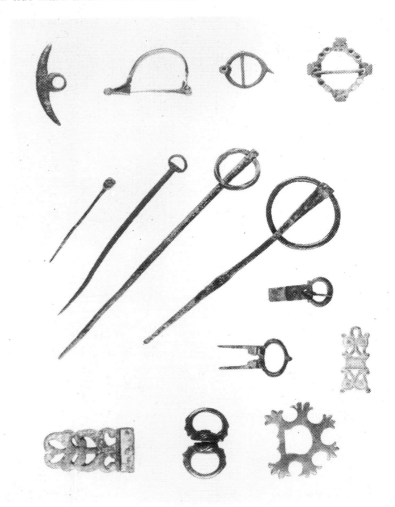

29.
Meols artefacts. Courtesy Grosvenor Museum, Chester.

Several hypotheses have been put forward, in an attempt to explain the quantity and variety of artefacts at Meols. Thus, a 'floating museum' could have been wrecked and its treasure floated ashore. Alternatively, the objects may have originally been connected with Chester and floated down stream. The antiquities may have been from a treasure chest, bought by Wiliam III's soldiers in Chester, and left behind after their departure to Ireland.

The most acceptable explanation is the existence of an ancient coastal settlement, and the preserving effect of peat bog. At one time the coast must have extended further seaward than at present.[38]

The Meols site was vividly described by E.W. Cox who visited the shore in 1895. He noted the remains of circular stone huts, up to two feet below high-water mark, made of wattled wood coated with clay, and the ground 'was abundantly marked with the hoofs of horses with round shoes, and with the foot-marks of cattle, pigs and sheep...'[39]

When I visited the Meols shore in the spring of 1982, layers of peat bed were clearly visible and, in places, vegetation and tree life. In the last century, and until about the 1930's, remnants of tree trunks from the submerged forest were visible at low-tide. Like the ancient settlement at Meols, the submerged forest was lost to the tides. The Irish Sea claimed one of Wirral's most important and fascinating historical sites.

30.
Submerged forest at Meols, c.1922. Courtesy Wallasey Reference Library Collection.

Fig. 5.
Old Cottage at Meols, c.1910. (Drawn by Shirley Robinson and based on an old photograph in the possession of Mr. A. Egerton).

51

Fig. 6.
Corbel in the Great Hall, Birkenhead Priory. (Drawn by Shirley Robinson).

Chapter III

Birkenhead, Bebington and Bromborough

(i) BIRKENHEAD

In a discussion of old Birkenhead, one inevitably ends up talking about the Priory. Before the nineteenth–century, there is really very little to talk about. Birkenhead is essentially a product of nineteenth-century town planning, and its growth due largely to the establishment of a steam ferry service on the Mersey in 1821.

At the turn of the eighteenth-century, Birkenhead township - exclusive of Claughton and a small part of Oxton - possessed 110 persons, an ancient priory, a ferryhouse and a handful of cottages and houses. Fifty years later there were over 8,000 inhabitants, only one quarter of whom were natives of Cheshire.

Philip Sulley described the early history of Birkenhead as 'meagre in detail, and limited in extent.'[1] There is no mention in Domesday and, as a settlement, Birkenhead was probably non-existent until the monastery was established there in the twelfth-century.[2] At least until the middle of the seventeenth-century it was part of Claughton.

The name of the township is thought to derive from the birch trees which apparently grew in abundance in earlier times in this part of Wirral, hence Birkenhead or headland of birch trees. An alternative theory suggests that the name might derive from the River Birket, the stream running across North Wirral and out into Wallasey Pool. This is highly unlikely, for the Birket only appears in documents and maps from the mid nineteenth-century. In mediaeval documents Birkenhead appears as *Birket-wood* or *Bircheved.*[3]

31.
Birkenhead Priory, 1780. Courtesy Williamson Art Gallery & Museum, Birkenhead.

THE PRIORY OF ST. JAMES

Nestling beneath the towering cranes of a nearby shipyard, a short distance from the Mersey Tunnel, lies one of Wirral's most important historical sites. The precise date of Birkenhead Priory's foundation is unknown but most authorities agree on the second half of the twelfth-century. This assumption is based primarily on the Norman work in the chapter house.

There may be some link between the existence of an important river ferry and the foundation of a priory. The Rule of these Benedictine monks was very much based on practical principles and it is unusual for a religious house to be placed in what was then a very remote corner of Wirral. The right of electing their own priors seems to suggest that the monks had independence.[4] However, John Leland (writing in the sixteenth-century) described the priory as a 'celle to Chester.' If it had been attached to the Abbey of Chester there would have been more surviving records.

The Prior of Birkenhead was evidently a figure of some local importance and influence. He claimed certain exemption and privileges, such as freedom from attendance at the Hundred Court of Wirral. This was quite a bonus, as the mediaeval round of litigation was both onerous and persistent. The Prior was also engaged in activities further afield; in 1288-9 for example, he represented the religious houses of Cheshire at an important meeting in Chester when disputes over the fairs were settled between the Abbey and the City. In 1379 the Prior witnessed a deed at Warrington relating to the friary there.

Before Wirral was disafforested, the Chester Forest Rolls show that the monks were frequently in trouble with the foresters especially as they claimed special rights and privileges.

In 1354 the Prior had to substantiate his right to several of these privileges. He claimed for himself, the monks, their convent and beasts, common pasture in Bidston, Moreton, Saughall Massie, Claughton and Tranmere, and rights of exemption from forest jurisdiction and the Hundred Court.[5] The Priory 'held practically all modern Birkenhead except Oxton, Higher and Lower Tranmere and the part of Higher Bebington which is now within its extended limits.'[6]

The monks' grange, or farmlands, stood between what is now Alfred Road and Euston Grove. An ancient road called Grange Lane (now Grange Road) ran eastwards to the priory. The grange actually occupied land in the old township of Claughton, hence the former name of Claughton-cum-le-Grange.[7]

A granary, or warehouse, was established in Liverpool (the Rumford Street end of Water Street) where the monks stored produce that remained unsold on market days.[8]

By the end of the fifteenth-century, Birkenhead Priory was no longer prosperous. In 1496 there were only five monks and the house was exempted from clerical taxation on the grounds of poverty.[9] Between 1518 and 1524 the Priory was visited several times by the king's commissioners. On each occasion they found everything very much in order; 'no suspect women had access to the house and no boys slept in the dormitory.'[10]

On the eve of the Dissolution of the Monasteries (1534), the Priory and its lands were assessed at just over £102 with debts of £12. The lands, with values, were as follows:

Grange lands, 'Birket Grange', water mill and ferry boat	£9	0s.	0d.
Moreton	£3	4s.	5½d.
Claughton	£5	0s.	4d.
Tranmere		17s.	0d.
Heswall		3s.	4d.
Barnston			8d.
Higher Bebington			4d.
Saughall Massie		11s.	0d.
Upton		3s.	0d.
Davenham (near Northwich)		4s.	0d.
	£19	4s.	1½d.
Lands in Lancashire (Warrington, Newsham, Liverpool and Melling)		15s.	2d.
(Total temporal income)	£19	19s.	3½d.
Bowdon Church	£45	7s.	6d.
Half of Wallasey Rectory	£14	3s.	8½d.
Bidston Church	£10	19s.	8d.
Backford Church	£12	6s.	8d.
(Total spiritual income)	£82	17s.	6½d.
(Total gross income)	£102	16s.	9½d.
Less charges for lay steward, bailiffs and estate managers, pensions and payments	£12	3s.	10d.
(Total net income)	£90	12s.	11½d.

We might compare this net income with that of Norton Priory, near Runcorn (£180 7s. 6½d.) and Chester Abbey (£1030 5s. 6d.)[11]

An Act of 1536 granted to the king, outright, the property of all the lesser monasteries (including Birkenhead) with an income of less than £200 a year. The Prior, John Sharpe, received a pension of £12 a year but he had to pay this back if he took up a benefice of that value or more.[12] The Act gave the Prior and the monks the choice of accepting a dispensation to leave religion altogether, or else be transferred to another religious house. Some of the monks may have moved to Wallasey or Bidston churches or, further afield, to Chester.[13] The average pension of an ordinary monk was about five or six pounds a year. In the years 1540-50 this represented the wage of an unskilled workman.[14]

After the Dissolution, the Priory was managed by the royal bailiff until March 1544 when Ralph Worsley obtained a grant for £568 11s. 6d. Worsley was a member of King Henry VIII's household, Steward of Chester and Keeper of the Lions in the Tower of London.[15] In 1544-5 the lands were valued at £115 3s. 5d. and included holdings in Bidston, Woolton (a 'lost manor' near Claughton), Claughton, Moreton, Saughall Massie, Wallasey, Seacombe, Tranmere, Bebington, Bromborough, Heswall, Upton, Backford and Davenham. In addition, the priory estates included the rectory of Wallasey, Bidston, Backford and Bowdon churches, and property in Chester (chiefly the Hospital of St. John the Baptist, on a site near Northgate, destroyed in 1644).

After the death of Worsley in December 1573, the priory lands passed to his daughter Alice, who married Thomas Powell of Husley in Denbighshire. Powell, who died in 1628, was responsible for a new house on the site of the old Guest House (west of the priory remains, now occupied by a school). This was dismantled in 1644 when the priory buildings were occupied and garrisoned by Parliamentary forces, but rebuilt in 1706. In 1843, after further additions and alterations 'it was entirely demolished and the gardens laid out for streets, some of which are already covered with upwards of one hundred shops and houses.'[16]

In 1710 John Cleveland of Hinckley, Leicestershire - M.P. and Mayor of Liverpool in 1703 - bought the properties which subsequently passed to the Price family through the marriage of his daughter.

THE SOUTH-WEST VIEW OF BIRKENHEAD PRIORY, IN THE COUNTY OF CHESTER

32.
Birkenhead Priory, 1727. Courtesy Williamson Art Gallery & Museum, Birkenhead.

THE PRIORY BUILDINGS

The natural beauty which may have attracted the monks to this once-remote site has long been lost. The remains of the priory are now hemmed in by a modern shipyard and industrial estate.

The history of the buildings, after their sale to Worsley in 1544, is rather obscure. The church was probably destroyed at the Dissolution; all that remains is part of the west wall of the north transept, although the complete triple arcade on the north side of the church existed in the eighteenth-century. This was destroyed when the new Church of St. Mary was built in 1819.

The chapter house is probably so well preserved because it was used as a domestic chapel after the Dissolution, at least until the new church was built in 1819. By this time, the other buildings had fallen into ruin and the growth of ivy contributed to the loss of much early stone and woodwork.

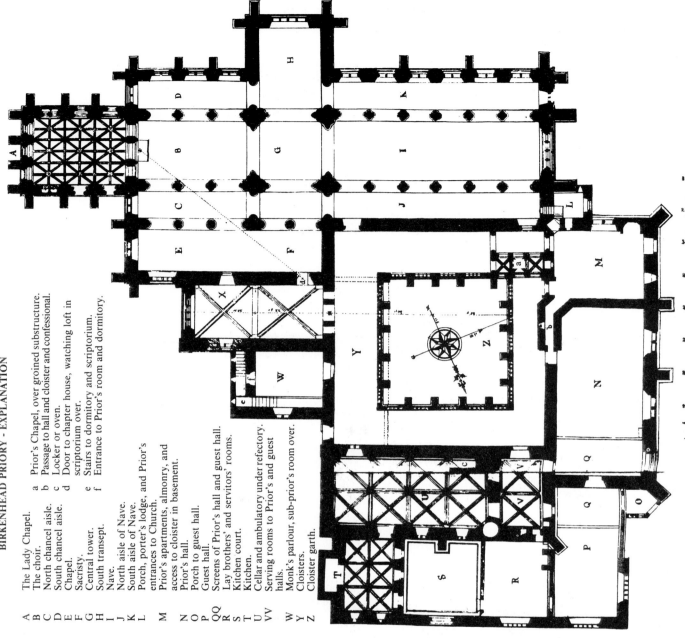

BIRKENHEAD PRIORY - EXPLANATION

- A   The Lady Chapel.
- B   The choir.
- C   North chancel aisle.
- D   South chancel aisle.
- E   Chapel.
- F   Sacristy.
- G   Central tower.
- H   South transept.
- I   Nave.
- J   North aisle of Nave.
- K   South aisle of Nave.
- L   Porch, porter's lodge, and Prior's entrances to Church.
- M   Prior's apartments, almonry, and access to cloister in basement.
- N   Prior's hall.
- O   Porch to guest hall.
- P   Guest hall.
- QQ   Screens of Prior's hall and guest hall.
- R   Lay brothers' and servitors' rooms.
- S   Kitchen court.
- T   Kitchen.
- U   Cellar and ambulatory under refectory.
- VV   Serving rooms to Prior's and guest halls.
- W   Monk's parlour, sub-prior's room over.
- Y   Cloisters.
- Z   Cloister garth.

- a   Prior's Chapel, over groined substructure.
- b   Passage to hall and cloister and confessional.
- c   Locker or oven.
- d   Door to chapter house, watching loft in scriptorium over.
- e   Stairs to dormitory and scriptorium.
- f   Entrance to Prior's room and dormitory.

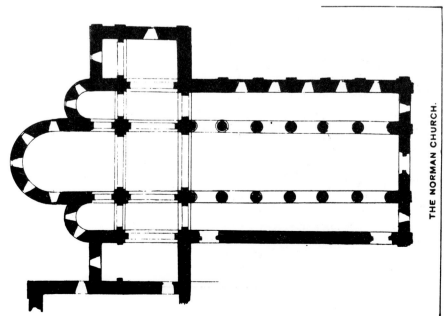

THE NORMAN CHURCH.

NOTE.—The line of orientation passes through the centre of the plan, through door of chapter house and the Prior's seat in chapter house, and through Prior's place at the dais of this hall. The east front is planned to present seven gables towards the river; and the east front three gables, the west two gables, and the south two gables—seven in all in these three fronts. In the cloister court five gables. The deviation of the orientation is one point of the south of east—east-south-east. One of the diagonal groin ribs in the ambulatory has been inadvertently omitted.

Fig. 7.
*Birkenhead Priory recovered plan from E.W. Cox, 'Birkenhead Priory', T.H.S.L.C., N.S., X,
(1894).*

In 1896 the Historic Society of Lancashire and Cheshire, with the support of the Birkenhead Literary and Scientific Society and the Chester Archaeological Society, set about acquiring the priory remains and, ultimately, the site came came under the care of Birkenhead Corporation.[17]

The buildings are arranged around a quadrangle and the layout is unusual in that the priory church was placed on the south and the cloisters are on the north. This arrangement is similar to that of Chester Cathedral, and may be due to the need for shelter from the south-westerly sea breezes.[18]

The chapter house is the finest surviving specimen of Norman architecture in Wirral. At one time the room was divided by a partition, and the groove marks are still visible on the north and south wall. The chapel is lighted by three windows, two of Tudor style and a third (on the south side) of Norman origin. In the south-east corner of the chapel is a mediaeval grave slab, inscribed with the name of a prior who died in 1473.[19] This was discovered during restorations and, after some time in the external wall of the chapter house, it was moved to its present position in 1913.

33.
Chapter house, interior.

34.
Chapter house, exterior.

35.
13th century doorway, west range.

The room above the chapter house - traditionally called the *scriptorium* - is probably early fifteenth-century in origin. There is a large fireplace on the south side which is similar in design to the one in the prior's apartments, and the corbels (supporting blocks) for the old tie-beams of the roof still remain.

The western half of the chapter house was linked to the church by an archway (now filled in) and to the quadrangle by the doorway which still remains between two windows.

To the north-east of the chapter house is the site of the dorter range, or monks' sleeping accomodation. The range of buildings on the north side of the quadrangle, north-west of the chapter house, may have been the monks' dining hall.[20] The sub-vault, often referred to as a crypt, may have been used for the accomodation of 'inferior' guests and is divided into a larger and a smaller room. In the smaller portion was the buttery or serving room. From here a circular stair leads to the room above, and a doorway at the east end led to a separate apartment for the sub-prior. In the walls of the smaller room are three recesses, or cupboards.

The western side of the priory - that facing Priory Street - is late thirteenth-and early fourteenth-century work. In the northern bay there is an elaborate external doorway. The 'great hall' was probably used for receiving 'superior' guests. For example, King Edward I is known to have paid two visits to the priory, in September 1275 and August 1277.[21] This hall was separated from the serving lobby by a large fireplace, of which a corbel remains in the west wall.

36.
Guest hall.

The hall has its axis north to south, possibly to shelter the cloister and also so that the prior's apartments, in the southern end, could adjoin the church. The southern range was of two storeys; the prior's lodging and chapel were reached by steps in the north-east corner and, in the south-east corner, the prior had access to the church. In the south wall of this upper level is a fireplace, further east a two-light square headed window and, next to this, two corbels which were part of a series which supported the floor above. On the west side of the quadrangle is the prior's own door. According to Mr. C. Aldridge, writing in 1890, the arms of the priory were carved over it.[22] In the nineteenth-century, the south end of the western range was found to be insecure and was dismantled and rebuilt using the original masonry.

Until the 1950's a graveyard existed to the south-east of the priory remains and this is now covered by dockland.[23]

37.
Western range of priory.

THE FERRY

The creation of Liverpool as a borough in 1207 must have provided a stimulus to the Priory's trade, especially as there were no restrictions on markets. Inevitably, the Priory became a stopping-off place for travellers across the Mersey and for troops going to Ireland, via the Dee and Wales.

The shelter of travellers must have become rather burden-some, and in the early fourteenth-century the Prior complained to the king's council that the priory buildings were inadequate for this purpose. A royal licence was issued on 20 November 1317, allowing the monks to build sufficient houses.[24] In 1318 King Edward II (1307-27) gave his consent to the Prior to purchase and sell food to travellers.

The king granted further rights to the priory in April 1330 when he made over the right of the ferry and, furthermore, the right to take reasonable tolls.[25] This royal charter may have merely regulated a long-standing tradition, for the ferry must have been in existence before 1330.

It is rather interesting to note that our mediaeval ancestors thought the ferry tolls were excessive! In 1354 the Prior was summoned before the court of the Earl of Chester and had to justify the high charges. The Prior claimed that he charged twopence for a man, whether laden or unladen, and a horse; one farthing for a man on foot; a half-penny for a man (unladen) and one penny for a man (laden) on market days at Liverpool.

In 1357 the Prior had once again to defend his ferry claims by producing his licence of 1318 and grant of 1330. The Earl of Chester claimed that by building houses to accomodate travellers, the game in the forest was threatened. The problem of high ferry tolls was again discussed. The dispute was settled in May 1358 in favour of the Prior.[26]

'Woodside' probably originated from the 1317 grant of land and lodging. In 1536 the profits of this ferry (as opposed to the original monks' ferry) were valued at £4 6s. 8d. a year and were leased to Ralph Worsley. In the 1550s he fought a legal battle with the lord of Tranmere, who had established a 'rival' ferry at Seacombe, over the loss of valuable rights.[27]

The present Woodside landing stage dates from 1826, and is some 100 yards to the west of the old 'quay' site. This consisted of large boulders, and at low tides the passengers waded out or rode on the ferrymen's backs.[28] The ferry-house was situated on the north side of Tranmere Pool (a tidal creek now absorbed by shipyards) and the old toll-house on land now occupied by the Royal Mersey Yacht Club.

The original monks' ferry was probably some 400 yards south of the present Woodside stage, on a site taken over illegally by the Monks Ferry Company in 1838. Further south, the Birkenhead Ferry was established in 1819.

The prosperity of Birkenhead in the nineteenth-century was due largely to the existence of a river ferry and, as Ronald Stewart-Brown wrote in '1925, 'the Woodside ferry may almost be said to have governed the fortunes of the place from ancient to modern days.'[29]

(ii) BIDSTON

Bidston is a delightful historical haven; an architectural anachronism basking in a sea of suburban sprawl. The silver sandstone buildings blend into a glorious homogeneous whole and - in this combination of old architecture and mellowed stone - one is tempted to compare it to the sort of timeless village found in the Cotswolds.

The survival of this almost intact mediaeval village is due rather to persistent campaigning than to any long term conservation policy. Only in comparatively recent times was Bidston designated a Conservation Area, in order to halt the progress of a modern housing estate.

Originally, the parish of Bidston comprised Bidston, Moreton, Saughall Massie, Claughton and Birkenhead - almost the whole of North Wirral but not quite up to the coast. The parish is not mentioned by name in Domesday, but it could be the 'seven hides' which Hamon de Mascy (Massey) held in the great manor of Eastham.

38.
Bidston Village, from the west.

The last of this Massey line died in 1334 and the Bidston estates (which also included Dunham, Bowdon, Altrincham and Hale) passed to Oliver de Ingham. Ultimately, they passed to Roger Lestrange (d.1349) who, with the assistance of the Earl of Derby, bought off Hamon de Mascy's heirs.

On 24 June 1397 John Lestrange, who inherited the lands in 1382, sold the manor of Bidston to John Stanley of Lathom, ancestor of the earls of Derby. Stanley was responsible for the creation of a deer park in 1407, covering some 160 acres.[30] This lay on the west side of Bidston Hill, between the village and Ford, and parts of the enclosing stone wall still exist near the observatory.[31]

The manor stayed in the Stanley family during the sixteenth-century and in 1507 the yearly value was £48 5s. 1d. In 1521, due to the wardship of Edward, third Earl of Derby, the manor was held by lease.

It is likely that the Stanleys came to Bidston for recreation, and used Bidston Hall as a hunting lodge. In 1572 we know that Thomas Egerton, solicitor-general and one-time Lord Chancellor, was appointed Master of the Game at Bidston by Henry, fourth Earl of Derby. He was granted five marks a year for life, with an annual entitlement to one buck and one doe.[32]

Henry was succeeded in 1593 by his son, Ferdinand, who also resided at Leasowe Castle in Wallasey.[33] He died suddenly in 1594 and was succeeded by his brother William.

39.
Old wall, Bidston Hill.

William became known as 'the wandering earl' on account of his European travels, and he is sometimes mentioned in connection with Shakespeare's plays. The Stanleys were great patrons of play-acting in Chester and the Chester Mystery Plays and Midsummer Shows relate, in some aspects, to Shakespearian drama. The suggestion that it was another 'W. S.' who wrote the plays is fascinating but unlikely.[34]

William Stanley was probably responsible for the refurbishing of the Hall. After about 1617, but more especially after the death of his wife in 1627, the Earl was a frequent resident and sought a peaceful 'retirement.'[35] After this time, also, the Bidston estate was handed to William's son and heir, James, Lord Strange.

James was executed by Cromwell's forces in October 1651 and the Bidston lands were seized by parliament. Ultimately, the lands (worth £250 a year in 1640) were restored by the Crown and passed to Sir Robert Vyner in 1680.

About the year 1820, Bidston became separated from its smaller townships. In 1801 Bidston had 199 inhabitants, Birkenhead 110. By 1831 Bidston, with 252 inhabitants, had become a rural retreat whilst Birkenhead, boosted by the sea trade, became a 'little suburb' of Liverpool with 2,569 people.

Today, Bidston Village still retains an old-world air and aspect of 'quaint restfulness,' although somewhat tainted by a nearby housing estate. Albert Smith's description of 1847-8 is still valid:

'It was a little quiet, grey village - so very grey,
indeed, and venerable, and quaint, that no flaunting
red brick had dared to show itself and break the
uniform tint of its gabled antiquity.'[36]

'Stone Farm' on the corner of School Lane, opposite the church, was once the 'Ring O'Bells' inn which sold its last flagon in 1868. In the eighteenth-century it was an important part of the smuggling network in North Wirral.[37]

Almost opposite Stone Farm is the largest farmhouse in the village called Church Farm. A tradition states that this seventeenth-century building once housed a group of monks. There are at least two distinct phases of building; the facade and the varying levels of mullions.

40.
Church Farm.

THE CHURCH OF ST. OSWALD

Although the present building is largely a nineteenth-century recreation, there is some evidence that a church occupied this site from at least the twelfth-century. Bidston Church formed part of the endowment of Birkenhead Priory, thought to have been founded about 1150, and it is also mentioned in a papal taxation charter of 1288-91. The church dedication is modern (1882) but is thought to recall a mediaeval bell inscription.

Before the rebuilding of 1855-6 there was a 'very fine Early English (nave).'[38] This description, along with that of Ormerod and Sir Stephen Glynne, suggests that an aisled church with a nave of three bays stood on the site in mediaeval times, the arcade surviving until 1855.[39] Alterations, chiefly to the windows, were carried out in the seventeenth-century and in 1854 plans were drawn up to remedy the 'unsound state' of the church. According to Thomas Helsby in his 1882 revision of Ormerod, the 'general features' of the older edifice were followed during restoration work. Much of the older masonry was re-used, but a fourteenth-century style was adopted for the window tracery and other architectural detail.

A stone built into the gable of the porch, dated 1593, is said to have come from a position over the old south doorway. This probably recorded some rebuilt portion.

The most intriguing aspect of the church is the west doorway which features a series of eight carved panels set between two corbels. Five of these panels contain heraldic shields and insignia. They help us to date the tower, together with its general architectural character which is late-Perpendicular.[40] Evidence of the maunch gule (or cut-off leg) in the sixth panel suggests that the tower was built before the death, in 1521, of the second Earl of Derby. His wife was a daughter of Edward. Lord Hastings of Hungerford whose emblem was the maunch.

62

41.
West doorway (Church of St. Oswald, Bidston).

From left to right, the panels feature a lion passant (denoting the Strange family who, as we have seen, where lords of Bidston after Massey), an eagle's leg (Lathom badge), the legs of Man (the Earls of Derby were the Kings of Man 1407-1771), a maunch, and a fleur-de-lys (Massey?). If this interpretation is correct, the shields may well represent a heraldic history of the manor of Bidston.[41]

All the church fittings date from the period of rebuilding (1855) or later. The registers begin in 1679, although for the period 1581-1679 they can be supplemented with those of the Bishops' Registry in Chester.[42] The churchwardens' accounts begin in 1767.

42.
'The Lilacs' c.1910. Courtesy Birkenhead Reference Library Collection.

Adjacent to the church lies the building called 'The Lilacs,' formerly known as the vicarage and, at one time, John Carey's farmhouse. The interesting features of this seventeenth-century house include the chimneys, stone copings and mullioned windows, although the fabric has been allowed to degenerate. The tithebarn is probably contemporary with the house, which one authority claimed was built in 1670.[43] In recent years there have been plans to convert these dilapidated properties to a restaurant and, in another application, residential flats. The Lilacs remains the blight on Bidston, despite council and conservation bodies' concern.

Across the road from The Lilacs stands Yew Tree Farm, dated 1697. This quaint cottage of oak beams and flagged floor used to be topped with a thatched roof.

43.
Yew Tree Farm.

As we continue on our tour of Bidston Village it may be as well to remember that, in former times, the road was much wider than today. There used to be a wide open space called the 'goose green' with a pinfold (where stray cattle where kept), stocks, and - in the nineteenth-century - a wheelwright's shop. This open space covered the land now occupied by the war memorial, but extended further westwards.[44]

BIDSTON HALL

Just up from Yew Tree Farm lies Bidston's crowning glory, at the east end of the village and on the north-west slope of Bidston Hill. Several factors suggest that this small manor house was built in the early years of the seventeenth-century, possibly on the site of an earlier building.

The layout of the house, with terrace, forecourt and gateway, and central hall is typical early Jacobean. We know that there was a 'goodly house' at Bidston in 1616 and that the Earl 'enlargeth the convenience therein for his pleasure and abode many ways.'[45] This suggests rebuilding and must be seen in the context of a general trend during this period.[46]

There is some evidence that Henry, fourth Earl of Derby, and his wife, may have used a house at Bidston after their marriage in 1555.[47] The evidence of masons' marks on the external stonework also suggests an earlier building. The mark also appears on the Elizabethan part of Stonyhurst in Lancashire (built 1588-96) and in almost the same position on both buildings.[48] Henry was very friendly with Sir Richard Sherborne, the builder of Stonyhurst. It may be that, during alterations to Bidston Hall in the 1620's, older masonry - from an earlier construction - was used.

The entrance to the hall is through an old archway topped by stone mouldings, which have variously been described as wine flagons or inverted glasses. There is a legend that the hall changed hands, in the seventeenth-century, over a game of cards and - as if to confirm this - an old summer house which stood to the north-east was built in the shape of an ace of clubs.[49]

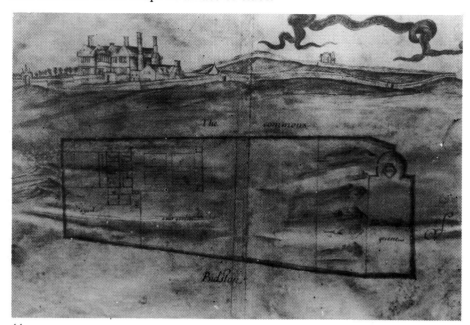

44.
Bidston Hall, 1665. Courtesy Birkenhead Reference Library Collection.

Bidston Hall evidently possessed four parallel gabled roofs, containing attic rooms, in the seventeenth-century. These were removed in the nineteenth-century and, at the same time, the chimneys were lowered.[50] The porch shows Renaissance influences in its design and opens directly on to the central hall. This has a flagged floor, but the fireplace is modern. The two front rooms, at the north and south end of the building, (formerly the kitchen and parlour respectively), have been completely modernised. The present kitchen occupies the whole of the south end of the building.

45.
Bidston Hall, interior.

A stone stairway leads to the upper floor, where there are eight rooms the largest of which is over the hall. Originally, there was one large room over the hall. The two rooms at the north end preserve the original arrangement of the ground floor, that is with a passage in between.

E1.

At one time the eastern face of the Hall, the loggia or recessed walk, was blocked up. It has now been restored, and it has been suggested that this may have once formed an open piazza for the performance of plays. The cellar has been called an 'underground dungeon' and was probably entered by a ladder.

In the eighteenth-and nineteenth-century, the Hall was used as a farmhouse and unfortunately the alterations by successive tenant farmers robbed the house of nearly all its internal architectural features.

The present form of the house is due largely to the efforts of the late Harold 'Max' Faulkner, in the late-sixties. The restoration of Bidston Hall, by this time rotten and neglected, was Faulkner's labour of love. Although primarily interested in old buildings, Faulkner campaigned for the preservation of our heritage 'a one day vital link with our English character and way of life' and wished to conserve Bidston's charm and history. Faulkner's ideas were summarised in his self-financed dossier, *Appeal For Survival,* published in June 1971. This is a fascinating manual of initiative and enterprise, and should be read by anyone interested not only in Bidston, but in the preservation of our heritage generally.

46.
Bidston Hall, exterior.

(iii) WOODCHURCH

The old parish of Woodchurch was nearly 5,000 acres in extent and included nine townships - Woodchurch, Landican, Noctorum, Arrowe, Oxton, Thingwall, Barnston, Pensby and Prenton - as well as parts of Irby, Upton and Claughton. There is no mention of Woodchurch in the Domesday Book, but a priest is given for Landican.

Landican - the name might refer to Tegan's Church (recalling some little known British or Welsh saint) - was probably the original manor and settlement from which Woodchurch developed.

The advowson of Woodchurch probably rested with the Norman barons of Nantwich. It subsequently passed to the Praeus family of Bartomley, south-east Cheshire, and, in 1350, to the Fouleshursts of Crewe. The lands remained in their possession until 1540.

THE CHURCH OF THE HOLY CROSS

The present church dedication is modern but may recall the Celtic saint, Tecwyn, Tegwyn or Tegan, whose festival was September 14, also Holy Cross Day. A late thirteenth-century deed actually mentions the Church of St. Peter, Woodchurch.[51]

The site of the church now presents an aspect of leafy tranquility amidst the hue and cry of a modern housing estate. The approach to the church building is lined with yew trees. It was customary in mediaeval times to plant these trees in churchyards in order to supply archers with wood for their bows. The outer arch of the porch has those peculiar deep indentations found elsewhere in Wirral, which may result from the sharpening of arrows by the archers.

The south porch is sixteenth-century with an original oak door. In a recess to the right of door is the remains of a holy water stoup. In each wall of the porch is a small window which contains fragments of mediaeval glass removed from the windows of the church. These depict the letters 'EP' and a cherubic face, and the heraldic arms of the Fouleshurst family who acquired the Woodchurch lands in the fourteenth-century.

While the north aisle is modern, the south aisle is separated from the nave by low arcading bearing the date 1584. The north wall of the chancel has been called Norman. There is a single lancet window over which has been set an early wheel cross. According to one of the former rectors, this wall 'contains some of the oldest masonry in the county' but, as Fred Crossley pointed out, 'it bears unmistakable evidence of being later and may be the result of restoration meddling.'[52]

47.
South porch (Church of the Holy Cross, Woodchurch).

48.
Lancet window and wheel cross (Church of the Holy Cross, Woodchurch).

49.
Mediaeval poppy-head (Church of the Holy Cross, Woodchurch).

The basic twelfth-century building has been disguised by the subsequent addition of arcades, a chancel arch and window. These changes probably took place in the fourteenth-century, when the south aisle was added and a west tower. In the early sixteenth-century the south aisle was remodelled and the south porch added. The church underwent major restoration in 1824 and 1844, when part of the east side was rebuilt and the tower cased due to bad weathering of the original stonework.

Built into the north-west and south-west corners of the tower are two buttresses. On the south-west there is an inscription, dated 1675, probably referring to the churchwardens of the time. There is also a scratch dial, a vertical sun-dial of mediaeval origin.

Of the interior fittings, the chancel stalls contain four carved bench ends said to be the finest mediaeval woodwork in Wirral. The decoration includes heraldic devices, acrobats and roses and oak leaves and acorns. The font, a sixteenth-century octagonal stone bowl, stands beneath the tower.

At the back of the south aisle hang the picturesque bread shelves on which loaves were placed each Sunday for distribution to the poor. Each rack bears an inscription with the name of the benefactor. Thomas Gleave, citizen of London, gave £50 in 1641.

Entrance and Garden Front, Tranmere Hall.

Fig. 8.
Tranmere Hall from J.Mayer, 'On the Old Halls of Cheshire No.1 : Tranmere Hall',
T.H.S.L.C., Vol.III, (1850-1).

The known rectors of Woodchurch date from 1264 and the complete list (from 1286) can be seen on sandstone tablets on the west end of the nave, either side of the tower. The parish registers begin in the year 1571 for baptism and marriage, and 1580 for burials. However, there is a break in the list of baptisms between 1618 and 1624 and in the weddings from 1609 to 1663. The churchwardens' accounts begin in 1763.

The present rectory was built in 1861 on an older site. In the cellar there is a datestone inscribed '1631 R.D.' possibly recording a former rector.

(iv) TRANMERE

Tranmere is not mentioned specifically in the Domesday survey but some authorities believe it might be Sumreford, included after Greasby and Storeton. In the late Middle Ages, one half of Tranmere was in the possession of Robert Holme, ancestor of the family who collected the famous Cheshire Papers now in the British Museum.[53]

Until the nineteenth-century, Tranmere was only second in importance to Neston. From the Bebington parish registers it is possible to chart the growth of the village. In 1600 Tranmere accounted for only nineteen per cent of birth and burial entries compared to Bebington. By 1650 this proportion was twenty three per cent.[54] In 1801 the population was 353 compared to Neston (1,486) and Birkenhead (110).

Tranmere originally consisted of two parts; Hinderton, a fishing village which stood near the junction of Hinderton Road and Green Lane, and the village proper centred upon Holt Hill lying between Rodney Street and Downham Road. A third hamlet, Watts Heath, lay near the present Heathfield Road.

For such an important old village, it is rather sad that there are no physical remains of the past with the exception of the restored cross. Tranmere's showpiece was the Old Hall 'pulled down by an ignorant boor...to make way for shops and houses.'[55] The Hall and its grounds covered about 1½ acres and looked onto Church Road and Greenway Road. The road, Tower Hill, now occupies the centre of the site.[56]

50.
Tranmere cross.

In 1818 a visiting Londoner described Tranmere Hall as 'a very ancient *brick* building much out of repair.' This is something of a paradox, for we know that the use of brick as a building material only became widespread in the latter half of the seventeenth century. Fortunately we possess the description of Joseph Mayer who considered that the Hall was 'not remarkable for any external display or architectural features.'[57] He mentioned an ornamental doorway with a 1614 datestone and a 'curiously' decorated window in one of the main rooms. Tranmere Hall was demolished in 1861.

Tranmere's churchyard cross was discovered in 1935 in the grounds of the New Hall, (demolished in 1936), where it had become a sun-dial and garden ornament. The pillar and base were reset on steps near the Church Road entrance to Victoria Park.[58] Philip Sulley described the cross (in 1889) as situated in Church Road near the junction with Dial Road.

(v) BEBINGTON

The modern borough of Bebington was created in 1937. Before this time, the area consisted of several small communities; Lower and Higher Bebington, Poulton-Lancelyn, Storeton and Tranmere. The name Bebington is thought to signify the homestead of an Anglo-Saxon chief, 'Bebba.' Although not listed in Domesday, the manor is first mentioned in a late eleventh-century charter when the lands were held by the Lancelyn family. Bebington - and the adjacent Poulton - remained in their hands until the sixteenth-century, when they passed by marriage to the Greenes of Northampton.

Higher Bebington has been called 'a hotch-potch of mean and featureless cottages' and Mortimer (1847) described the houses of Lower Bebington as 'very insignificant.' Apart from the splendid church there is little left of antiquity.

At Number 25, The Village, near the Rose and Crown pub, is the oldest council house in Wirral. At one time the building was two cottages sharing a thatched roof. The gable of the eastern end (facing The Grove) 'is a good example of the late type of timber framing prevalent towards the end of the seventeenth-century.'[59]

51.
Cottage at Bebington.

The western part features an upper chimney piece with the date 1653. The cottage contains eighteenth-century alterations and, internally, the eastern part has been heavily modernised.

A 'great' hall may well have existed in Lower Bebington Village in mediaeval times, possibly associated with Chester Abbey. During the widening of the road leading south-west from the centre of the village, in 1897, mediaeval fragments were discovered.[60]

THE CHURCH OF ST. ANDREW

Raymond Richards in his seminal work *Old Cheshire Churches,* published in 1947, wrote that 'Bebington possesses what is undoubtedly the finest old parish church in Wirral...'[61] Nathaniel Hawthorne, the American author and one-time U.S. Consul in Liverpool, thought that St. Andrew's was the perfect example of an old English village church. He was not so impressed, however, upon a second visit when creeping ivy had started to take its grip on the steeple.[62]

Bebington parish church is perhaps so impressive because it is a splendid amalgam of building styles. From the simple Norman arcades to the magnificent Tudor work in the chancel, the church epitomises the nature of English ecclesiastical architecture.

After the Conquest, the advowson of Bebington was granted to the Abbot and Convent of St. Werburgh who held it until the Dissolution. After this time it passed to the Stanleys of Hooton and, in the seventeenth-century, to a branch of the Poole family.

In early times, St. Andrew's was called Whitchurch (or White Church) probably to distinguish this silvery stone building from the more usual timber structure of the period. Restoration work in the nineteenth-century seemed to confirm a local tradition that a Saxon church occupied the present south aisle of the nave. The masonry below the foot of the south nave wall is probably Norman. The original nave of the Norman church consisted of four bays, of which two arcades remain (the most westerly).[63]

Towards the end of the thirteenth-century, the Norman south door and porch were dismantled. In the 1320s the nave was extended north, and the Norman chancel removed. Fragments of this were evidently re-used, notably in the west end arches. Some of this masonry also found its way to local gardens. From a close examination of the surviving fragments, Mr. E.W. Cox described a Norman church with a nave of four bays and a chancel of two bays each possessing a north aisle.[64]

71

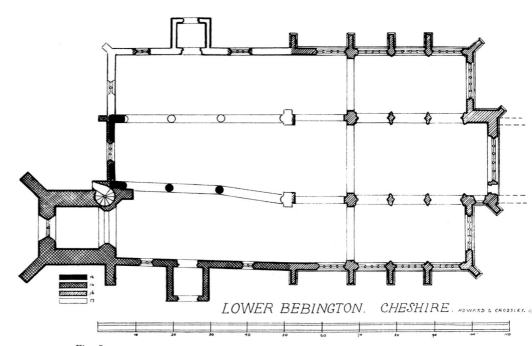

LOWER BEBINGTON. CHESHIRE. HOWARD C CROSSLEY.

Fig. 9.
Plan of Bebington Church from F.H.Crossley, 'Cheshire Churches in the Twelfth Century', J.C.A.S., N.S., XXXII, Part II, (1938).

A second chancel was built in the fourteenth-century. The nave remained until 1847, when the north wall was altered to build a new north aisle, and a new south arcade was constructed. The door, porch, and the two original side windows of the nave were reset in this new arcade. At the same time, the ancient cradle-framed roof of the nave was destroyed. Only the western wall of the c.1320 nave remains in the original position. The tower - one of three surviving mediaeval spires in Cheshire - was built in the early fourteenth-century.

The last mediaeval addition to the church was the chancel of three bays, with its two side chapels forming chancel aisles. This has been called 'one of the finest compositions to be found in its style in any local parish church.'[65] The fourth bay formed the crossing where a twelfth-century tower once stood. It is clear that the whole church was going to be rebuilt from the east, but the scheme stopped abruptly probably as a result of the Dissolution. The old Norman bay was set against the 'new' (late-Perpendiculiar) nave. The masons' marks, 'more numerous than any in Wirral,' and most noticeable in the chancel and chapels, suggest that a large number of men were employed in this project.

52.
Norman arcade (Church of St. Andrew, Bebington).

The proportions of the windows in the chancel, in particular the interior face of the east window of the south aisle, have been called 'perfect in shape and design.'[66]

In the eastern end of the chapels there was once a north and south door. The southern door, still visible from the outside, led to the priest's lodgings. This 'annexe' was used as a school from 1635 but was destroyed in 1840.

The roofing of the church is almost entirely modern; the original roof of the chancel was destroyed in the 1897 restorations, and some of the oak was used for panelling and tables.

Sadly, St. Andrew's has lost many of its ancient fittings. Several windows possessed mediaeval stained glass, but this was probably destroyed in the 1847 restoration along with a number of grave cross slabs. A mediaeval grave slab has been set on the wall of the south aisle, above the arch of the nave at the west end, and two exist below the benches in the south chapel.

The only known relic of the mediaeval church floor is a tile, once housed in the Mayer Museum, discovered in a garden near the church.[67] The parish chest, at the west end of the nave, is thought to be mid sixteenth-century. In the tower vestry is a charity bread board dated 1641. The font, which is based on an octagonal pillar, is probably Norman in origin. The three choir stalls in the chancel have been 'sadly mutilated' and almost entirely reconstructed. The decoration includes a pelican, a bearded face and a dolphin. There are four oak bench-ends with mediaeval tracery.

54.
East window (Church of St. Andrew, Bebington).

73

53.
Church of St. Andrew, Bebington, from the south-east.

The remains of the churchyard cross, a sixteenth-century base, is now situated near the north porch, while the fourteenth-century headstone is incorporated in the stone seat of the south porch. A cross-head and part of the shaft - thought to have come from the pre-Norman church - are now in Bebington Public Library.

The parish registers begin in 1558, and the churchwardens' accounts date from 1775. The list of known rectors goes back to 1294 and their names are inscribed on a carved board inside the church.

(vi) POULTON-LANCELYN

Poulton Hall has for three centuries been the home of one of Wirral's oldest families, now known as Lancelyn Green. They claim descent from Scirard who about the year 1080 gave, to Chester Abbey, the chapel of Bebington, the tithes of the manor, and land in Cheshire, Derbyshire and Dorset.

In the later thirteenth-century, William Lancelyn granted the Abbot three butts of land in Poulton to enclose and use as a grange and cottage.[68] He also granted the Abbot permission to build a bridge on land between Bromborough and Bebington.[69]

There are probably two generations missing between Scirard and the earliest known Lancelyn of Poulton. The Lancelyns were probably the heirs of Roger, under-tenant of Poulton, who - in 1086 - married a daughter or grand-daughter of Scirard.

In the Middle Ages, the Lancelyns were a Wirral family of some importance; they held courts in Poulton, Lower Bebington and Little Meols, owned lands in Pensby, Leighton and Larton, and claimed certain forest privileges.[70]

By October 1569 Elizabethan Lancelyn, daughter and heir of William Lancelyn the sixth (who died 20 August 1550) had married Randle Greene. The Greenes were a Northamptonshire family; Maud Green, a member of one family branch, was the mother of Henry VIII's sixth wife Catherine Parr, while Graham Greene, the novelist, can trace his descent from another branch, the Greenes of Greene-Norton. From this branch the Lancelyn Green's derive their crest, the three stags.

55.
Poulton Hall, from the west.

The present hall was probably built for Roger Lancelyn, who was also responsible for the 'family tree' drawn up in 1654. It is an elegant, two-storeyed building and probably occupies the site of an earlier structure. Ormerod described a former hall that stood on a 'high knoll' - presumably a reference to the ancient castle which, until the early twentieth-century, was marked on maps. This occupied a defensive position to the north of the present hall in the fields known as the Marfords.

The oldest portion of Poulton Hall - L shaped in appearance - is mid seventeenth-century although the rough cast exterior disguises the antiquity. On the first floor, in the room known as 'The Dark Attic,' is a section of wattle and daub.

The outbuildings include a seventeenth-century brewhouse, now partly used as a scout meeting place. It gives us a better idea of the original appearance of the hall.

Poulton is sometimes referred to as Poulton-cum-Spital, on account of the small neighbouring hamlet of Spital. As the name suggests, there was a lepers' hospital here in the Middle Ages on the site of Spital Old Hall. There may also have been a chapel dedicated to St. Thomas the Martyr and commemorated in the valley known as Chapel Dale, also one of the reputed sites of the chivalrous adventures outlined in the poem, *Sir Gawain and the Green Knight.*

In 1174-84 the Archbishop of Canterbury confirmed the possessions of the Chapel of Thomas the Martyr including plough land, half of the site of a mill and a fishery.[71]

56.
Old family chest, Poulton Hall.

(vii) BROMBOROUGH

The name Bromborough (mediaeval *Brunburgh*) is thought to derive from the personal name, Brun's stronghold. Alternatively, the brun element may refer to a well or spring. At one time there were three wells in the area. St. Patrick's Well, in Brotherton Park off the Spital Road, is the legendary site of the Irish missionary landing in the fifth-century. The Petrifying Well, at one time also in Brotherton Park, may have been associated with the leper hospital at Spital. St. Chad's Well, in Shodwell Wood, is now hidden beneath a power station.

The history of Bromborough has, unfortunately, been coloured by myth and legend. There is absolutely no factual evidence for the existence of a monastery here in Saxon times.[72] The Battle of Brunanburh could have been fought in one of several places but most probably in the country lying between the Ribble and the Mersey in Lancashire. In 937 Aethelstan, King Alfred's grandson, defeated a combined army of Danes, Irish, Scots and Welshmen. The site of this outstanding victory has never been properly established and Bromborough's claim largely rests on its position overlooking the Mersey. The Danish fleet, under King Anlaf, sailed from Dublin and we know that in the tenth-century there was a strong Norse population in Wirral.[73]

In 1847 a number of damaged skulls and the iron head of a spear were discovered under the old nave floors of St. Andrew's Church, Bebington. Might these have been remnants of the Battle of Brunanburh? It is nice to romanticise, but the historical reality is less evocative.

William Webb, writing in *The Vale Royal of England* (published in 1656), mentioned a chapel at Bromborough and this existed until 1828. Ormerod (1819) described the original structure of this building as largely Norman, but by the early nineteenth-century it was in such a 'wretched state of dilapidation' that it had to be demolished. Philip Sulley recorded that 'no real effort at restoration was made.'[74]

During excavations preceding the building of a third church, in 1863-4, some of the carved stones of the ancient structure were discovered. In 1909 these stones had become 'an inartistic pile in the rectory garden' and were subsequently put inside the church. Many of these fragments disappeared during rebuilding, although pieces of a Saxon cross were incorporated in the restored church cross east of the south porch of the present church.

It appears that, at the time of the Domesday Book, Bromborough was the 'mother' church to Eastham.[75] In the mid twelfth-century the church, and the manor house, was presented to the Abbot and Convent of St. Werburgh. The estates later passed to Sir Richard Cotton, Bishop Bridgewater and James Mainwaring of Chester.

In April 1278 Edward I granted a weekly market to the monks of St. Werburgh's, in their manor of Bromborough, and a yearly fair lasting three days.[76] The old market cross - the steps and base are ancient - now stands in the centre of the village.

The manor house of the monks was situated just north of Pool Lane and west of the old Court House. The three remaining sides of a moated enclosure are still visible and this defensive position on the edge of Bromborough Pool may have been to repel Welsh invaders, and forest outlaws. The buildings were accidentally destroyed by fire in 1284.[77]

Preliminary excavations of the moat were conducted in 1955 by members of The Bromborough Society. An excavation by Liverpool University Rescue Archaeology Unit in 1979 produced no evidence for the construction of the moat before the eighteenth-century. This suggested that the present line of the north moat is not mediaeval, but the result of later re-working.[78]

Close to this moated area is the site of the Court House, a late seventeenth century building pulled down in 1969. For many generations this was the house of a Chester family, the Hardwares.

> 'The house is one long unit with a wing protruding
> forwards at each end, it is the stone verged gables of
> these wings which form...the dominate feature of the house.'[79]

There were three storeys and a loft, and three original chimney stacks. The western end of the house was probably a nineteenth-century extension and the farm outbuildings were probably late seventeenth-century in origin. The site of

the Court House is now encircled by chemical pipes, a mausoleum of ivy, moss and bracken. Only an old wall and several large pieces of masonry reflect former inhabitation.[80]

Bromborough Hall, demolished in 1932, was early seventeenth-century with later alterations. It occupied a site just across from the church, near the present Royal Oak pub. The Manor House Farm, which disappeared in 1930, stood to the south-west of the Cross, at the junction of Allport Lane and The Rake. It was 'an interesting house of stone and brick, decorated with armorial designs and a date tablet marked 1676...'[81] The house contained some interesting carved blocks which formed part of a mantelpiece in an upper room. These carved stone beasts, probably dating from Elizabethan times, were rescued from a garden in West Kirby and placed in the grounds of Stanhope House.[82]

57.
Court House Farm, Bromborough (above) and Court House site in 1968 (below). Courtesy Unilever PLC.

58.
Manor House Farm, Bromborough. Courtesy The Bromborough Society.

59.
Stanhope House, Bromborough.

Stanhope House, at the corner of Mark Rake and Spital Road, was built in 1693 and was once known as 'Spann's Tenement' after its one-time owners.[83] It is a red sandstone building with mullioned windows, gables and three storeys and a loft. The porch is modern and was added when the house was converted to a public library in 1939. At the same time the ground floor was completely altered and the floors of the upper storeys removed. The original oak panelling to the drawing room was removed but later the room was restored using panels from Chillingham Castle, Northumberland. The chimney stacks show eighteenth-and nineteenth-century additions.

The surrounding garden wall possibly pre-dates Stanhope House on account of the several stones with deep indentations. These marks are found elsewhere in Wirral and they may well result from archers sharpening their arrows before target practice. The street name Mark Rake is also indicative.

The preservation of Stanhope House and, in general, the conservation of Bromborough as a historical centre, is largely due to The Bromborough Society founded in May 1933.

Several old cottages and farmhouses existed in Bromborough until the early twentieth-century. One of two still remain. Pear Tree Cottage (No. 6, The Rake) bears a 1699 datestone but the roof is now slated and the walls whitewashed.

60.
Mark Rake, Bromborough.

Fig. 10.
Bromborough Market Cross. (Drawn by Shirley Robinson).

1.
Submerged forest at Meols in 1982.

2.
Old dining room, Leasowe Castle.

3.
Bidston Village, showing Stone Farm and Church of St. Oswald.

4.
The crypt or undercroft, Birkenhead Priory.

Chapter IV

Villages of Wirral

(i) GREASBY

At the start of the twentieth-century, Greasby was an agricultural village with a fortnightly cattle market, and a population of 290. Today, Greasby is a 'commuter suburb' with over 7,000 inhabitants. This dramatic transformation is a comparatively recent phenomenon and stems largely from the introduction of public motor transport after the first world war, and the decentralisation of population in the Merseyside region.

Many families, and newly-married couples, were attracted to the semi-rural atmosphere of the area. However, despite the campaigning of local protest groups, Greasby has become 'merely another segment of the ever-spreading suburbia generated by the needs for housing of Liverpool and Birkenhead.'[1]

At the time of the Conquest, *Gravesberie* was held by a certain Dunning who may have been a 'greave' or high official of the earls of Mercia, and who also held Storeton. At one time it was thought that the place name of Gravesberie derived from the Anglo-Saxon *graf* or grove, and so referring to the woodland that once covered the area. A more probable derivation is from the words *graef* and *byrig* signifying a fortified house with a pit or trench.

Sometime before the Domesday survey of 1086, the manor was given to Nigel de Burci, and the value was less than in 1066. Prior to 1093 the Greasby tithes, along with those of Storeton, were given by Hugh Lupus, first Earl of Chester, to the Abbey of St. Werburgh in Chester. Subsequently, Robert de Rullos conferred the entire township on the abbey and the charter was confirmed by his sons, Richard and Robert, in 1284-5.[2]

After the dissolution of St. Werburgh's Abbey, in 1540, Greasby was granted to the Dean and Chapter of Chester Cathedral. In 1556 the estates passed to Sir Richard Cotton, privy councillor and controller of the king's household, and his son George. In the seventeenth-century, Greasby was held by Edward Glegg of Irby (1657).

61.
Greasby Old Hall.

Greasby still possesses some old buildings, and most of these are near the old village crossroads. Few retain period features. The Old Hall lies on the eastern side of Pump Lane and is almost hidden by outbuildings. Over the porch is a weathered coat of arms and the old oak entrance door still exists. The house has been much altered over the centuries, although oak beams and a large fireplace remain in an attic room. The eastern wing was probably added in the late seventeenth-century.

The Hall is said to have belonged to the monks of St. Werburgh, at least until the Dissolution. Recesses in the porch may have been used for monastic alms. A priest hole in the hollow stone wall of the room to the right of the porch, (now blocked up), suggests that the house was used as a hiding place for Catholic recusants in the seventeenth-century.

Most people know Manor Farm as a restaurant. The farmhouse and outbuildings date from the late seventeenth-century, and the granary bears a 1695 datestone.

School Farm, in Mill Lane, formed part of the estate of William Glegg, and was given by him to Calday Grange Grammar School in 1636.

Pump Lane, near the centre of the old village, takes its name from the old village pump which stands near the junction with Frankby Road.[3] It is often thought that this lane might be part of a 'Roman' road which extended from Chester, northward to Meols. 'Operation Pump Lane' in 1980-1 revealed no Roman construction although excavations by Peter France in 1964, south-west of Rigby Drive, uncovered forty large red sandstone kerbstones.[4] However as W. Thompson Watkin pointed out in 1886, '...the whole of the evidence as to a road from Meols to Chester is most unsatisfactory.'[5]

(ii) FRANKBY

Frankby is a village where the horse population almost outnumbers the human. The place manages to retain the 'rural' atmosphere and unhurried calm which near neighbour Greasby has now lost. A report published in 1973 by the Cheshire County Council Planning Department, noted that Frankby was unique amongst Cheshire villages in that the majority of inhabitants still gained employment from the surrounding farmland. By 1983, Frankby possessed only one working farm.

At the time of Domesday, Frankby was probably that portion of *Calders*, or Caldy, held by a Frenchman - hence the name of Frenchman's homestead. From the early twelfth-century, the manor was held by the Orreby family (who also held Willaston) and later it passed to the Ardernes and the Bold family of Lancashire, who held it from 1431-1612. After this time the holdings were sold to tenants, the principal of whom was Peter Day (who died in June 1641).[6]

The historical interest of the village lies in the old farm buildings clustered around the 'pocket handkerchief' village green. The village itself 'is surrounded by one of the best preserved open field enclosure patterns that remain in the district.'[7]

62.
Frankby village.

84

Don't be fooled by the impressive looking 'Tudor' mansion called Hill Bark. Although built on the site of an ancient tithe-barn at the summit of Frankby Hill, the building is actually 'Bidston Court' - a pseudo-Elizabethan edifice moved wholesale to this site from Noctorum and re-erected in 1929-31.

(iii) IRBY

In his book *The Wirral Peninsula,* published in 1955, Norman Ellison commented that 'Irby has lost its old-world charm and has become a suburb of Birkenhead.'[8] Irby Hall, therefore, looks somewhat incongruous. The present building is of early seventeenth-century origin and occupies the site of a manor house of the monks of St. Werburgh. Three sides of a moat are still visible.

Ormerod (1819) described the Hall as a 'plaster and timber building' but by 1888 the structure was 'rapidly falling into decay.' It was then restored but the half-timbering above the ground floor was not totally replaced. The remaining three sides are of stone, and a massive chimney-stack remains on the north side.

63.
Irby Hall, prior to restoration, c. 1888. Courtesy Birkenhead Reference Library Collection.

Irby Farm, at the village crossroads, was once the residence of an old Irby family, the Balls. Their tenancy of this farm can be traced back at least to the reign of Henry VI (1422-61). Various house plates on the outbuildings and main farmhouse refer to reconstruction work in the seventeenth-and early eighteenth-century.

64.
Irby Hall.

The mediaeval mill at Irby occupied a position to the south of Hill Bark Road. The first known reference to its existence is a late thirteenth-century taxation roll of Pope Nicholas IV. At this time the mill was owned and worked by the monks of St. Werburgh who acquired Irby township in 1093.[9]

Between about 1709 and 1725 the mill was probably moved to a new site to the north, immediately adjacent to the south-west corner of the Mill Cottage (now a public house). This later mill was demolished in 1898.[10]

(iv) STORETON

In early times Storeton may have been a place of some strategic importance, the 'hub' of a network of ancient roads and in sight of the surrounding land and sea coast.[11] The best known example of such an old track is 'Roman Road', sometimes referred to as 'Monks' Stepping Stones,' and stretching from Storeton to Woodchurch. This is almost certainly mediaeval in origin, a simple packhorse track stone-ribbed so that the locals could negotiate the muddy fields.[12]

Storeton Hill has been called 'one of the most picturesque features of Wirral' - a deep, solid ridge of fine white stone which has resulted from the faulting of the overlying strata of new red sandstone. The extensive quarries are now filled in and actually lie in the township of Higher Bebington. They once supplied fine quality stone to local builders. Several inscribed and sculptured Roman stones, now in the Grosvenor Museum, Chester, are thought to have come from Storeton and the stone was used at Bebington parish church, Birkenhead Priory and Storeton Hall.

At the time of the Domesday survey, Storeton formed part of the estates of Nigel de Burci, a retainer of the baron of Halton. About the year 1120 Storeton, with Puddington and the bailiwick (i.e. the area under official jurisdiction) of the forest of Wirral, was presented by the third Earl of Chester to his steward Alan Sylvester.[13]

The only daughter of Alan Sylvester's son, Ralph, married with Alexander, the tutor of the sixth Earl of Chester, and their daughter, Agnes, married Sir Thomas Bamville in 1315. Bamville's son and heir, Sir Philip the elder, had no issue so the estates were divided between Bamville's three daughters, the eldest of whom married Sir William Stanley. His great grandson was the immediate ancestor of a long and distinguished line of Stanleys.[14]

65.
Storeton Hall.

STORETON HALL

Although now incorporated, and almost lost, amidst a large working farm, Storeton Hall was once an important private residence. It was the seat of the Sylvesters, the foresters of Wirral under the Earl of Chester, then the home of the Bamvilles and, in 1282, the Stanleys who held it until 1848.

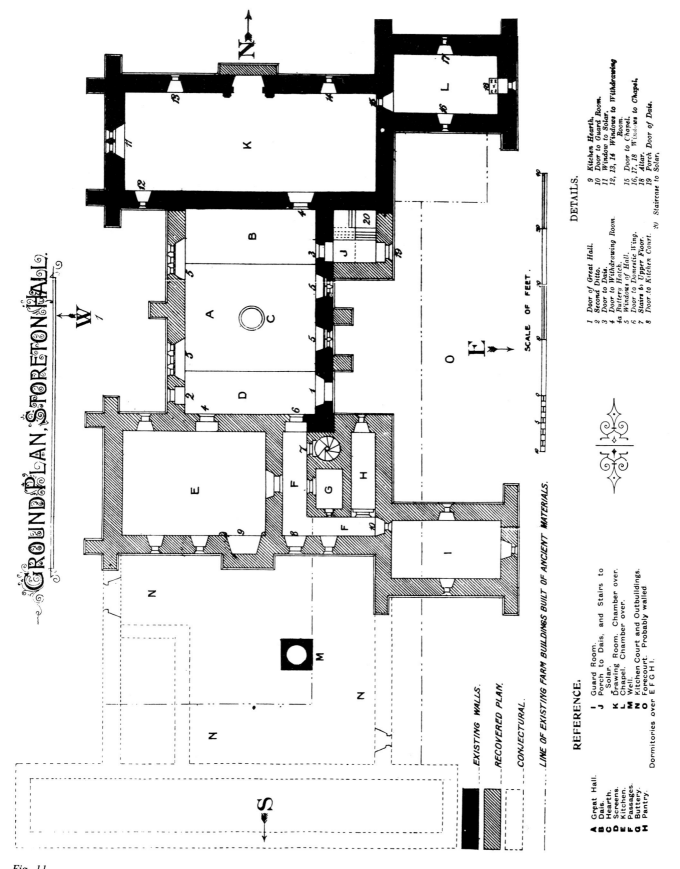

GROUND PLAN, STORETON HALL.

DETAILS.

1	Door of Great Hall.	9 Kitchen Hearth.
2	Second Ditto.	10 Door to Guard Room.
3	Door to Dais.	11 Window to Solar.
4	Door to Withdrawing Room.	12, 13, 14 Windows to Withdrawing
4a	Buttery Hatch.	Room.
5	Windows of Hall.	15 Door to Chapel.
6	Door to Domestic Wing.	16, 17, 18 Windows to Chapel.
7	Stairs b, Upper Floor.	18 Altar.
8	Door to Kitchen Court.	19 Porch Door of Dais.
		20 Staircase to Solar.

REFERENCE.

A Great Hall.
B Dais.
C Hearth.
D Screens.
E Kitchen.
F Passages.
G Buttery.
H Pantry.
I Guard Room.
J Porch to Dais, and Stairs to
Solar.
K Drawing Room. Chamber over.
L Chapel. Chamber over.
M Well.
N Kitchen Court and Outbuildings.
O Forecourt. Probably walled
Dormitories over E F G H I.

SCALE OF FEET.

EXISTING WALLS.
RECOVERED PLAN.
CONJECTURAL.
LINE OF EXISTING FARM BUILDINGS BUILT OF ANCIENT MATERIALS.

Fig. 11.
Ground plan of Storeton Hall from E.W.Cox, 'The Antiquities of Storeton, in Wirral', T.H.S.L.C., N.S., XIII, (1897).

66.
Entrance to 'solar', Storeton Hall.

The mediaeval Hall dates from the mid fourteenth-century and may have ceased to be the principal seat of the Stanleys after the building of Hooton Hall (1487-89) for Sir William Stanley. It may have been abandoned as a residence after the building of the farmhouse to the north which incorporates a blocked up Jacobean window. Although the Hall was neither crenellated nor moated, the doors and walls were unusually thick and may have been designed with defence in mind.[15]

There was originally a central hall on the west side, of which only the inside face of the eastern wall remains. This is now the outside face of farm buildings. A great entrance door remains at the south end and a central buttress suggests that there was a central hearth.

At the southern end of the hall there was once a doorway which led to the kitchen and butteries. At the north east end of the hall an arched doorway (now a storeroom entrance) led to a staircase tower. Mr. E.W. Cox (1897) concluded that, in the absence of corbels and sockets in the existing hall walls for the roof timbers, the hall roof 'was of cradle form, of the early type...'[16] The roof of the solar and chapel was probably similar.

The great chamber and solar, or upper living room, and the chapel with a room over it, are the best preserved parts of Storeton Hall at the northern end. The great chamber is now divided into modern offices and the springing (where the arch rises from its support) of the gables remains.

In the solar, to the west, there is a high pointed gable window of two lights which is now blocked up. The entrance to this room is by a small door from the chamber above the chapel although, originally, it was entered by the staircase tower at the south east corner.

Both the chamber and the solar once possessed fireplaces in the centre of the northern wall; of the latter, a moulded hood can still be traced in the wall.

The chapel is a small room to the east of the north wing. The external facings and tracery of the windows - if these existed - have been destroyed, and blocked by an external staircase of seventeenth-century date. In 1371 the Bishop of Lichfield gave authority to William Stanley to establish an oratory (i.e. a place for private worship) in Storeton.

The remains of Storeton Hall are now almost forgotten; the growth of ivy on the west side can only weaken this once formidable structure and all the historic rooms are now neglected. On my last visit (in 1982) the solar was being used as a snooker room for farm workers, whilst the chapel had become a repository for rubbish.

One would hope that somebody has the foresight to save this significant historic site from dilapidation. The archaeological and educational potential must be worth pursuing.

(v) BRIMSTAGE

A short distance from the busy Clatterbridge exit of the mid-Wirral motorway, lie a group of straggling cottages scattered around a village green. Brimstage - in mediaeval times *Brunstath* - was once part of Bromborough and subsequently, in 1868, united with Raby to the parish of Thornton Hough. It was the original settlement of an old Cheshire family, the Domvilles, whose eldest line is now represented by the Earl of Shrewsbury.

The first of this family occurs in the reign of Edward III (1327-77) when they also held Oxton, Raby, and part of Mobberley in East Cheshire. In 1397 the manor estates - which now included Thingwall - passed in marriage with Margery Domville, second daughter and heiress of John Domville the younger, to Sir Hugh Hulse of Raby.[17]

The son of Sir Hugh, Thomas, inherited in addition to the Brimstage estates, part of the manor of Little Neston, the hamlet of Hargrave and land in Thornton. After the death of Thomas in August 1432 William Troutbeck acquired all the Domville lands, as a result of the minority of Margery Hulse to whom he married his son.

The estate passed to Sir John Troutbeck of Dunham who was slain at the Battle of Blore-Heath in 1460.[18] As late as 1877 Brimstage and Raby were subject to a Court Leet (a local manorial court dealing with petty offences) held under the Earl of Shrewsbury.

The Domvilles were a family of some standing in the Middle Ages. In 1275 the inquisition of the death of Robert de Montalt (the steward of Chester and lord of Brimstage, who died in 1162) showed that Sir Roger Domville held land in Brimstage and Oxton. He was a member of the county court and sat on many juries, in 1277, 1281, 1284 and 1289.[19]

In 1334 John Domville, possibly the grandson of Sir Roger, was in possession of Brimstage and Oxton but let other lands to trustees, notably in Thingwall and Barnston. In January 1340 he was appointed warden of the property of Vale Royal Abbey, founded by Edward I for the Cistercian monks, south-west of Northwich.

John Domville and his family were frequently in trouble with the courts. In the trailbaston court of 1353, John Domville and Richard Hough - listed as sergeants of the peace - were accused of hiding treasure trove which was found at Gayton by one of Domville's tenants. They failed to hand it over to the Earl of Chester.[20]

It was further claimed that Domville, Hough and Robert Poole, together with about thirty others, hunted upon many occasions with greyhounds in the forest of Wirral. They threatened the Abbot of Basingwerk's lay-brother at Caldy grange and forced him to give them food and drink. The goods, corn and chattels belonging to the Abbot were destroyed by the men's violence, and his horses, greyhounds and dogs were threatened.[21]

BRIMSTAGE HALL

67.
'The Cheshire Cat', Brimstage Hall.

In February 1398 Hugh Hulse and his wife, Margery, obtained a licence to build an oratory at Brimstage. This private chapel is traditionally thought to be the vaulted room at the base of the mediaeval tower. This interpretation arises from the supposition that because a room is vaulted it was used for religious purposes. There is no real evidence that this was the case at Brimstage and the vaulted lower storey is typical of the mediaeval tower house.

In the south-east corner of this room at Brimstage is a roughly cut corbel, said to be an early representation of the 'Cheshire Cat.' The figure looks more like a fierce Scottish Fold than a 'Cheshire,' although the mason may originally have intended to represent the red lion rampant - the Domville coat of arms. On one of the ceiling bosses there are three entwined fishes, the arms of the Troutbeck family who inherited the Brimstage estates in 1432.

68.
Vaulted room, Brimstage Hall.

The central portion of Brimstage Hall, on a north-south axis, appears to be of sixteenth-century origin; the north part is a later addition. One authority has suggested that the Hall 'has every appearance of having been a tower house, i.e. a compactly planned dwelling of the pele-tower type.'[22]

The tower at one time consisted of three storeys connected by a flight of stairs winding round a central pillar. The rectangular turret at the south-east corner contains garderobes (lavatories) and rises to the full three storeys. At the summit there are machicolations, or holes in the floor to drop missiles through. This projecting roof, supported on massive corbels, may have been used for beacon fires as part of an ancient signalling network from North Wales to Storeton Hill.

The site of the Hall was surrounded by a moat which is still faintly visible on three sides. In part of the garden, near to the tower, several bodies have been found laid out in such a way to suggest that this area may have been once used as a cemetery.[23]

Finds made in the 1890s during the building of the house, close to the eastern entrance gate, included human bones and carved stones. 'The discovery of graves, the character of the tracery (of the fragments), and the finding of a stoup suggest a separate ecclesiastical building, standing with its graveyard to the east of the hall.'[24]

69.
Brimstage Tower, from the south-east.

(vi) RABY

Raby Village - if we can call this scattering of buildings a village - is a little piece of unspoilt Wirral. About 1½ miles to the east there is 'one of the beauty spots of Wirral' known as Raby Mere. This picturesque stretch of water is now used for purely recreational purposes, although centuries ago there was an important water mill there.

Raby is the Norse term for a boundary village and this township may have formed the boundary between Saxon and Norse territory. At the time of Domesday, Raby was divided into two parts - one held by the Abbey of St. Werburgh, the other by William, the Norman baron of Halton. The whole of the township passed into the monks' hands sometime before 1135. There was a monastic settlement at Raby and at nearby Thornton Grange.[25]

In 1350 Robert de Raby, a descendant of the family who succeeded the monks as lords of the manor, held the custody of the Bridge Gate at Chester. The Sergeancy remained in the Raby family until the early-fifteenth century, when it was divided between the families of Norreys and the Hulses. The prime function of this office was to keep watch and maintain the entrance gates to the City of Chester. By 1432 the Troutbeck family held Raby (together with Brimstage) and the lands passed ultimately to the Earl of Shrewsbury.

70.
The Wheatsheaf Inn, Raby.

The main building of historic and architectural interest is The Wheatsheaf Inn with half-timbering and low beams. The 1611 datestone is said to have been discovered in the gable during alterations. Norman Ellison remembered the 'rather rough, bare interior with wooden benches and a deep inglenook (the bench beside a fireplace), and beer in blue-banded mugs.'[26] For better or for worse, the place is now haunted by suburban drinkers.

(vii) WILLASTON

In mediaeval times the Hundred of Wirral was called after Wilaveston, or Willaston, the small village in the heart of the peninsula. In the Domesday survey, however, there is no mention of Willaston as a separate village although the manor of Edelaue is thought to be commemorated in the present Hadlow Road.[27]

The settlement at Willaston goes back at least to Saxon times and the discovery of stone implements in the area suggests neolithic occupation. Further evidence of Willaston's antiquity is a stretch of apparently Roman road at Street Hey Lane. In archaeological excavations east of Hargrave Lane kerbstones were discovered similar to those found at Aldford, on the line of the Roman road from Chester to London.[28]

71.
The Wirral Stone.

The so-called 'Wirral Stone', at the junction of Hadlow Road and the Chester High Road, resembles an old mounting block of three steps. It has variously been described as part of a Roman survey of Wirral or the very meeting place of the Hundred Court. Its former purpose is quite clear, according to the tithe plan of 1848 where the stone is clearly marked as 'The Pissing Stone.'[29]

The manor of Willaston first appears in a deed of 1230, by which Fulco de Orreby gave the lands to his mother together with Upton and Frankby. The Orreby family originated in Lincolnshire and came to Cheshire in the twelfth-century. The manor passed to the Arderne family of Aldford, by the marriage of Fulco's niece, and was let to the Mainwarings of Warmincham.

The manor was held by the Trussels from the 1320s to the mid sixteenth-century, when it passed to John Vere, Earl of Oxford. He decided to parcel out the lands to freeholders, and this probably accounts for the large number of substantial farmsteads in the immediate district.[30] After his death, in 1562, the extensive estates were sold off and, ultimately, were acquired by Sir Christopher Hatton, captain of the Queen's Bodyguard and member of the privy chamber.[31]

In 1831 38 out of 48 families living in Willaston derived their livelihood from agriculture. With the coming of the railway (the branch line from Hooton to Parkgate opened in 1866) and the motor car, Willaston's rural isolation was threatened. Cheshire County Council and local residents have sought to retain the rural atmosphere and preserve the historic landscape, and Willaston was the subject of a 'pilot' conservation study in 1969.[32]

For those who want to see Wirral's architectural heritage embodied in one village, they could do no better than to go to Willaston. The village green, which formerly extended to the west, is almost completely surrounded by old buildings. This aspect has, thankfully, remained unchanged in nearly one hundred years. In 1889 Philip Sulley wrote that Willaston 'presents the finest collection of ancient and picturesque farmhouses in Wirral.'[33]

72.
Corner House Farm, Willaston.

CORNER HOUSE FARM

Corner House Farm is at the south-west corner of the green and originated as a square-shaped building of two storeys. Portions of the original mullioned windows remain, a large stone inglenook fireplace, and an external door to the north.

In the first floor room of the gabled stone part is a fireplace inscribed, JB AB 1637 TB EM, possibly a reference to John and Anne Bennett. Also in this room is a representation in plaster of St. George and the Dragon. These fittings may not be contemporary with the house; there was evidence of later brick work encasing the fireplace, during restoration, suggesting that it could have been moved from elsewhere.

73.
Corner House Farm, Willaston (showing old mullioned window).

74.
Old fireplace, Corner House Farm, Willaston.

Similarly, the plaster relief may not be an original feature. Nathaniel Hawthorne, writing in 1854, mentions 'a rude marble sculpture representing St. George and Dragon found over the fireplace of a cottage near Rock Ferry' and which, he believed, originated at Birkenhead Priory.[34]

There are sections of wattle and daub in the internal walls of the stone portion, although now plastered over. The brick part to the north of the house, and that behind the old part, was probably added in the late seventeenth-or early eighteenth-century. The front porch is a modern addition and the south chimney has been rebuilt.

Near to this chimney, a cannonball has been found embedded in the stonework while an old wall to the south has those deep indentations found elsewhere in Wirral.

The house has remained in the Pollard family for at least one hundred years and in March 1983 opened as a restaurant.

THE OLD RED LION

The Old Red Lion was described as 'the most attractive old hostelry in Wirral.' It was probably built in the late sixteenth-century as a private dwelling. In the eighteenth-century it was occupied as two cottages, and in the early nineteenth century it became an alehouse.

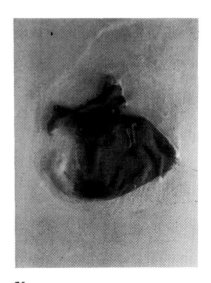

75.
St. George and the Dragon, Corner House Farm, Willaston.

76.
The Old Red Lion before restoration. Courtesy Birkenhead Reference Library Collection.

The widow of the last landlord (the public house closed in 1928) occupied the building until the late 1960s. In 1972 a Liverpool planner bought the property, after an unsuccessful attempt by the old Birkenhead Brewery Company to gain planning permission for a modern 'pub.' Restoration work was carried out during 1974 and to repair the timber frame the whole building was systematically dismantled and then rebuilt.[35]

77.
The Old Red Lion, Willaston.

The southern gabled part consists of two storeys each containing a single room. In the ground floor room there is a huge stone chimney-piece. The north part is older, and sections of wattle and daub were found in the external walls during restoration. The ceiling of this part has been raised to bring it into line with the central part of the building. The house plate may refer to John Bennett and his wife Marie, who married in 1608, and the date 1631 may signify the time of alterations to the gabled wing.

THE OLD HALL

This imposing building, south-east of the village green, has an Elizabethan-style facade. The stone over the front entrance featuring the date 1558, was actually carved in the nineteenth-century after restoration work uncovered an old chimney-piece in the main room on the first floor.

78.
Willaston Old Hall. Courtesy Ellesmere Port and Neston Borough Council.

Architecturally, the Hall is probably no earlier than 1600-20. We know that the Bennett family purchased a share of the Earl of Oxford's land in the late sixteenth-century, and the house remained with them until 1920.

The house is of three storeys with a central hall and large open fireplace. In the south room on the ground floor there is original oak panelling while in the main room on the first floor is the chimney-piece, already mentioned, which features the Bennett coat of arms and a frieze with flower ornamentation.

79.
Ash Tree Farm, Willaston.

ASH TREE FARM

The north wing of this farmhouse is dated 1697, but the strawberry red sandstone dressing and the style of building is very similar to that of the Old Hall. The oldest part is the southern half of the timber-framed portion facing Hadlow Road.

The original building consisted of a single room with a room above; a panel of wattle and daub in an upstairs room suggests at least a sixteenth-century origin.

The north wing has a house plate with the initials of former tenants, probably John Wilson and Elizabeth Tellett who married in 1693. The east wing is of brick in a timber frame.[36]

Home Farm, on the north side of the green, has been described as a 'good example of a Wirral seventeenth-century farmhouse.'[37] A house plate in the west gable bears the date 1616 and at the rear of the house is a brick barn. The buildings were used as farm dwellings until 1912; part of Home Farm is now used by a bank and part is a private residence.

The remaining buildings surrounding the village green are eighteenth-century; to the north Pear Tree Farm now partly used as a bank; to the west Laburnum Farm, and to the south Cherry Brow Farm.

80.
Home Farm, Willaston.

Chapter V

The Dee Estuary

(i) THE DEE PORTS

It is hard to imagine that the Dee estuary was once a busy thoroughfare for trading vessels on their way to and from Chester. In the Middle Ages the main sea trade of Chester port was with Ireland, and the chief import cargoes included grain and fish. Until about the mid fifteenth-century the main exports were salt and cloth. A small but regular wine trade with France and Spain continued until the late eighteenth-century.[1]

During the late Middle Ages there is evidence that Chester's importance as a sea port was declining.[2] The Dee estuary was silting up and ports were successively established further up the Wirral coast. In the early fourteenth-century, cargoes were discharged at the Red Bank (Dawpool) and subsequently at Shotwick, Burton, Neston and Gayton.

A petition of 1445, drawn up by the merchant traders of Chester, claimed that ships were unable to come nearer than twelve miles from the port. Again, in 1486, the Chester citizens complained that taxes were too high especially as the port was 'obstructed by the vehement influx of sand and silting up of gravel.'[3]

It would be easy to over-estimate the role of natural forces in the decline of Chester port; other factors were involved. The Hundred Years War with France, and poor relations with Spain, inhibited the wine trade. By 1575, Elizabeth I had granted a monopoly of the Spanish wine trade to the newly-established Spanish Company. There was the growth of Liverpool port which was better placed for the Lancashire textile trade.

Ultimately, Chester became an *entrepot* where goods were merely collected and then distributed. Much trade was in the hands of outsiders and local citizens derived little benefit from commercial activites and transactions. The Chester customs system may have been restrictive. Until 1559 it remained outside the direct control of central government, possibly because it was not big enough to justify inclusion in the national system.[4] Duties were levied by the chamberlain on wine, iron and leather, by the civic authorities on goods entering and leaving Chester, and there was a variety of other charges.[5]

By the late fifteenth-century there was no thriving harbour at Chester -the ancient 'Roode Eye' became 'a games field for horse racing and the prohibited game of football.'[6]

81.
Remains of the 'new key', Little Neston.

In an effort to revitalise commerce the Council of the City of Chester commenced the building of the so-called 'New Quay' in 1541. This was sited at Lightfoot's Pool, below Neston. Money which should have gone towards a new college at Chester was diverted to this scheme, and there was a series of local collections to help raise funds for the new harbour.[7]

Appeals for financial help to complete the quay continued until 1608, when the work was abandoned. This was due in part to lack of funds, but also the quay failed to accomodate the larger vessels. In 1779 it was partly demolished and the stone sold to Sir Roger Mostyn.[8]

(ii) WEST KIRBY

Until the late nineteenth-century, West Kirby contained the townships of West Kirby, Caldy, Grange and Great Caldy, Greasby, Frankby, Great and Little Meols and Newton-cum-Larton. Although not mentioned specifically in the Domesday survey, West Kirby was probably held by Robert de Rodelent (Rhuddlan) and part of the manor of *Calders* or Caldy. The survey mentions five distinct tenements and a Frenchman with a sergeant, who possessed two ploughs, possibly a reference to Frankby. The settlement was at one time called Kirkbye but became West Kir(k)by to distinguish it from Kirkby in Waley or Wallasey.

The name Caldy probably derives from the Old English, *cold arse,* a term which reflects both the shape of Caldy Hill and the exposed situation of the settlement. The existence of a separate Caldy Hundred in mediaeval records has long puzzled local historians. John Brownbill, in his book *West Kirby and Hilbre* (1926), suggested that it may be 'a partial survival of the semi-independent Norse colony permitted to settle here about 905,' and representing Robert de Rodelent's barony.[9]

THE CHURCH OF ST. BRIDGET

The church at West Kirby, and that of Hilbre, was given by Robert de Rodelent to the monks of St. Ebrulf, now St. Evroul, at Utica in Normandy about the year 1080. The estates were then sold to the Abbey of St. Werburgh, Chester, for an annual rent of 30s.[10] After the death of Rodelent, in 1088, they reverted to the earl of Chester who gave the church at West Kirby to his clerk, Nigel.

Ranulf Gernons, the fourth Earl (1129-1153), gave the manor of Caldy (including West Kirby) to his new abbey of St. Mary, Basingwerk in Flint. Great Caldy now occupies the eastern and northern slope of Grange Hill and contains the site of the monks' grange or farmlands. At the top of the hill was the ancient Grange Mill, destroyed in a storm of 1839, and now the site of the beacon pillar.

82.
Oldfield Manor Farm, Grange, (formerly New House, a 17th century building on the site of the monks' grange).

5.
Church of St. Andrew, Bebington.

6.
Church of St. Mary, Eastham.

7.
'Roman Road', Storeton.

In the late thirteenth-century there was a legal battle between the monks of Basingwerk and Chester. The Welsh monks thought that, as lords of the manor of Caldy, they should have the advowson of West Kirby church. In court proceedings at Chester they claimed that the post of rector had become hereditary, after the appointment of the Earl of Chester's clerk, contrary to the Lateran Council (1215) which forbade hereditary succession to churches.[11] Chester Abbey's claim was upheld; the Abbot of Chester had made the last presentation to office in time of peace.

In the Taxation Roll of Pope Nicholas (1291) the monks' lands were worth £8 16s. 8d. a year. By 1535 the manor of West Kirby and Great Caldy was worth £27 4s. 2d. In 1553 the Caldy Grange estate and monastic lands were sold by the crown to Richard Brooke of Newton and his wife for £1,343 10s. 10d., and later, in 1609, the manor passed from Richard's son, Thomas, to William Glegg, the founder of Cald(a)y Grange Grammar School.

83.
Hogback stone (Charles Dawson Brown Museum, West Kirby).

The church dedication suggests the existence of a pre-Conquest religious building. St. Bridget was a saint well known in Celtic lands and the dedication at West Kirby may owe something to the Norse-Irish colonisation of the area.

In the Charles Dawson Brown Museum near the church, and housed in an old schoolroom, there are fragments of cross-heads (c.1030) and two fragments of pre-Norman cross shafts. In addition, there is a hogback or memorial stone.[12] These pieces are typical of the Anglo-Danish and Anglo-Norse monumental art common in the north of England in the eleventh-century.[13]

From this archaeological evidence it may be concluded that the first *stone* church on the site was probably built in the mid twelfth-century. Evidence for a Norman church is provided by two architectural fragments -also in the museum - belonging to a doorway and a portion of an aisle.

Most of the mediaeval work remains at the east and west ends, although the upper part of the gable is modern. There is the base of an early thirteenth-century column at the west end of the north arcade.[14]

The east and part of the south wall of the chancel, the north chapel and vestry, date from the early fourteenth-century. The tracery of the great east window is similar to that found in some Irish churches, with its superimposed trefoils. While the west wall of the north aisle is mediaeval, the whole of the north wall was pulled down and rebuilt in 1869. On the south side, mediaeval masonry remains in whole or in part.

The embattled west tower, some fifty nine feet high, dates from the early sixteenth-century and has been described as 'a poor example of its period.'[15] Over the west doorway is a series of four heraldic shields alternating with rose-like ornamentation. The meaning is not clear.[16]

84.
Church of St. Bridget, West Kirby, from the north-east.

The plan of the church remained unaltered from the early sixteenth-century until 1789, when the north and south aisle were destroyed and the interior gutted. A new, single span roof was erected over the aisleless nave, chancel and chapel and 'the building returned to the chilling respectability of a Quaker meeting house.'[17]

In 1868 there were further proposals for an extensive restoration programme and an attempt to restore the church to its sixteenth-century plan. The 1869 work consisted mainly of the south aisle and south porch and a wholly rebuilt north wall using old masonry.

The church fittings are for the most part modern. The present font is of nineteenth-century origin but an early font (probably sixteenth-century) was dug up in the rectory grounds in 1893 and now rests in the nearby museum.

The only monument earlier than the eighteenth-century is that dedicated to Jan Van Zoelen of Bristol (1689), on the south wall of the chancel below the middle window. This Dutchman may have had some connection with William III's troops embarking to Ireland from Hoylake.

Next to the churchwardens' seats at the west end of the nave, on the inner faces of the tower buttresses, are two carved oak inscriptions taken from the old charity bread boards. The older one, on the north side, records the gift of Thomas Gleave in 1641. Four seventeenth-century oak benches are preserved; three in the baptistry and one under the tower.

The parish registers date from 1561-1619 and 1692-1729 (all entries). The Bishops' Transcripts at Chester can supplement these for the years from 1666. The churchwardens' accounts date from 1754 and the list of rectors begins in 1140 with Nigel, clerk.

86.
Seventeenth-century bench-end (Church of St. Bridget, West Kirby).

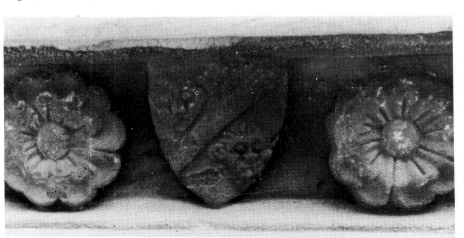

85.
Detail of west doorway (Church of St.Bridget, West Kirby).

(iii) HILBRE ISLAND

In mediaeval times Hilbre Island was a centre for shipping, conveniently situated at the head of the Dee estuary, and its importance increased in Elizabethan times with a regular flow of military traffic to Ireland. At an early date, possibly in the thirteenth-century, a beacon fire was established at Hilbre for the guidance of mariners and the Earl of Chester had to pay 10s. a year for its upkeep.

Hilbre - together with West Kirby - was formerly part of the manor of Caldy. The name commemorates St. Hildeburgh, a corruption of the seventh-century Mercian saint St. Edburge, and suggests a small religious house founded here before the Conquest. An early cross-head, now in the Grosvenor Museum, Chester, and a grave slab, in the Charles Dawson Brown Museum, West Kirby, indicates early Christianity. We know that a church existed at Hilbre before 1086 for it was given with the island by Robert de Rodelent to the French monks.

The monks of Normandy sold the island to Chester Abbey. For a time the Earl of Chester seized Hilbre and gave it to his clerk. In 1230 the Chester monks regained possession and retained the island as an outlying part of their parish of St. Oswald. They maintained a small cell, dedicated to the Virgin Mary, until 1536. The antiquary John Leland, writing in the 1530s, mentions 'a celle of monks of Chester, and a pilgrimage of our Lady of Hilbyri.'[18] A West Kirby man recalled, in 1575, that the Abbot of Chester maintained two monks continually on the island, who passed their time in prayer and fishing. The 'smallest traces' of this cell apparently remained in the nineteenth-century 'in a portion of the doorway and window built up in outhouses' and some flag-stones and the old monastery well.[19]

A mound along one side of the island, south-west of the present buildings, is said to mark the site of an ancient cemetery. It was here, in 1853, that a pre-Conquest cross-head was discovered and, in 1864, human remains and a late eleventh-or early twelfth-century grave slab.[20]

Excavations on Hilbre in 1926 - the most extensive to date - were rather inconclusive apart from finds of Roman and Romano-British vessels.[21] The so-called 'Monks' Bath' referred to by earlier writers was found to be no more than a hollow for deep rooted plants.[22]

87.
Hilbre Island.

It is clear from early maps that at one time Hilbre was a single island. The Hilbre group now consists of three islets making a total of 16½ acres; Great Hilbre, Middle Island or Little Hilbre and Little Eye. The islands are most widely known for their flora and fauna, a favourite with ornithologists and a Grade 1 site of Special Scientific Interest.

In winter and spring some 200 species of wading birds visit the islands; in the summer 500 people can walk out to the islands in any one day. A permit to visit is necessary (available from the local council offices) and careful timing is essential. The tide surrounds the islands approximately three hours before local high water and this means that they are isolated from the mainland for five hours in every twelve.[23]

From April 1974 Wirral Borough Council became custodians and the new Leisure Services Committee emphasised 'its determination to pursue a policy of safeguarding Hilbre against undesirable development.'[24] Although the uniqueness of Hilbre for the study of natural history has long been recognised, the historical and archaeological potential of the site has never been fully realised.

What Hilbre does lack is an ancient ruin to fire the romantic imagination and provide a focal point, such as the priory at Lindisfarne or the modified monastic ruin at St. Michael's Mount in Cornwall. Great Hilbre contains two groups of stone buildings and part of the Telegraph Station (1847) is said to contain remnants of a sixteenth-century inn.

(iv) THURSTASTON

In his account of Thurstaston published in 1923, F.C. Beazley wrote that the parish 'has no history, and...it almost seems at times as if a conspiring hand existed to stop us from learning anything about it.'[25] The derivation of the place name has been the subject of some controversy. The most likely explanation is that Thurstan's tun or farm, rather than 'Thor's Stone Tun' referring to the large natural formation on the Common. This latter idea received some currency in the nineteenth-century, after one writer described the legend of the stone as one of human and animal sacrifice.[26]

Thurstaston was given by Hugh Lupus, first Earl of Chester, to Robert de Rodelent and prior to this time the manor was held by the Anglo-Norse chieftain Leofnoth. In mediaeval times, Thurstaston was included in the Hundred of Caldy and after the death of Rodelent was given to the Montalt family who were lords of Mold and Hawarden. In the second half of the thirteenth-century the manor passed to the Haselwalls, through the granddaughter of Richard de Thurstaston, the grandson of Matthew de Rodelent.

In the fourteenth-century a dispute arose between the Whitmores, a Staffordshire family, and the Vernons and Athertons. The Whitmores claimed descent from David, the eldest son and heir of Sir Patrick Haselwall and his wife Agnes. A fine of 1325 stated that the manor of Thurstaston should pass either to the issue of Cecily, daughter of David de Haselwall, and her second husband William de Whitmore of Chester, or in default to Richard, son of Ralph de Vernon of Shipbrook. Both the Vernons and the Athertons claimed descent through Eustachia de Vernon who married David de Haselwall.

In 1369 Ralph de Vernon was implicated in an attempt to possess Thurstaston Hall by force. Several of the raiding party, which included William Stanley, the head forester of Wirral, and his brother, John, were armed with bows and arrows. They enticed a woman who was inside the house to go and call a bailiff and when she had left they shut the door and took possession.[27]

THURSTASTON HALL

Thurstaston Hall has the distinction of remaining in the same family for a least six centuries. It is, then, unique in Wirral and the present owner can trace his ancestry back to Robert de Rodelent. Philip Sulley (1889) mentioned an older hall of which considerable ruins remained in the early nineteenth-century and William Mortimer (1847) described a moated site.[28]

The central part of the present Hall, on a north-south axis, dates from the late sixteenth-century. The date and initials 1680 WWD probably refers to restoration work. There is a 'Tudor' fireplace and carved panels in the main entrance hall, possibly removed from the west wing, and in the east dining room over the mantelpiece are the arms of Glegg. The present owners, the Turners, married into the Baskervyle-Glegg family and inherited the property in 1914.

The west wing is mid fourteenth-century but one small room; to the rear of the house, may be earlier. In 1980 Gill Chitty and students from Liverpool University conducted a preliminary investigation, and she reported that this outhouse 'would certainly appear to be mediaeval in date and one of the earliest parts of the hall standing.'[29] It formerly had a vaulted ceiling.

88.
Thurstaston Hall.

Another room in the house is panelled entirely in oak and there are early polished oak beams in the 'Arch Room'. The east wing was built about 1835.

To the right of the entrance hall, at the foot of the main staircase, is a wooden figure reputed to represent Thurstaston's original benefactor, Hugh Lupus. However, a mid eighteenth-century account describes the statue as a representation of John Whitmore, mayor of Chester in the fourteenth-century.[30] The statue's garb is Cromwellian.

In August 1971 a gang of Water Board workmen stumbled across an old 'smugglers' tunnel whilst laying a new water main along a private road off Station Road. The tunnel appeared to run in the direction of Thurstaston Hall, perhaps from the old port of Dawpool.

It is not certain from what date the hamlet of Dawpool developed; the houses there had disappeared by the early nineteenth-century. It seems likely that Dawpool was an anchorage point in the Middle Ages and the Red Bank - mentioned frequently in sixteenth-century records - was situated on the shoreline of the Dee estuary at Thurstaston.

89.
Shoreline at Thurstaston.

The present church at Thurstaston, dedicated to St. Bartholomew, is the third known building on this site. Until 1724 the church remained inside the courtyard of the Hall. The first church, presumably Norman, may have survived until 1820. Daniel Lysons in *Magna Brittania* (1820) described 'a small church, with turret;

chancel, ancient, semi-circular; narrow window in the depth of the wall but not pointed.'[31]

The tower of the second building, (erected in 1824), remains. On the north side there is an old inscription said to have come from under a window on the south side of the first church. The present church was built in 1886 and all the fittings are modern.

The list of rectors, (on three tablets on the west wall), begins in 1303 and the first extant register begins in 1706. A transcript in the Bishops' Registry, Chester dates from 1581 although incomplete.[32]

(v) HESWALL, OLDFIELD AND GAYTON

Heswall, Domesday *Eswelle,* became the property of Patrick de Haselwall, Sheriff of Chester (1277) and subsequently passed to the Calveleys and Davenports and, in 1699, the Whitmores of Thurstaston. The parish originally comprised two hamlets, Heswall-cum-Oldfield and Gayton.

The Church of St. Peter, Heswall is a product of extensive restoration. Although the tower is fourteenth-century, the rest of the structure dates from 1879. This is the third known construction on this site; a second church of 1739 was destroyed in a great storm of 1875.[33]

90.
Mediaeval tower (Church of St. Peter, Heswall).

The tower has been described as having a 'chequered' appearance due to the replacement of the old stones with bricks. An inscription 'HD' towards the top of the south face, and a talbot or hound on the west face, suggests that Hugh Davenport of Calveley may have been responsible for the building, or restoration of the tower. He died in 1469.

Heswall and Woodchurch were unique parishes in Wirral, in that the churches were independent of any monastic institution. The parish registers begin in 1539 for marriages and 1558-9 for baptisms and burials, making this one of the earliest records of its kind. The earliest extant churchwardens' accounts date from 1778.

There are several early monuments in the church, at the base of the tower, commemorating the Glegg and Whitmore families. There is a memorial plate to John, second son of William Glegg of Gayton, who died in 1619.[34]

A manor house almost certainly existed in Heswall in mediaeval times. Ormerod (1819) described a hall to the north of the church, then occupied by farmers, with a moated site still visible.[35] In the eighteenth-century this building was called 'The Further Hall' and later 'Farr Hall', to distinguish it from nearby Gayton Hall. It occupied a site near the present Farr Hall Drive and the parish church.

91.
Oldfield Hall.

Oldfield is a small hamlet which adjoins Heswall and, in mediaeval times it was a separate manor given by Patrick de Haselwall to Guy de Provence. Guy may have been one of the knights in the service of Eleanor, one of the daughters of the Count of Provence, who married Henry III in 1236. He also obtained land in Pensby and Little Saughall.

Oldfield Hall used to belong to the Hooton Stanleys. Sir Rowland Stanley retired to the house towards the end of the sixteenth-century and died there in 1614, aged 96. Scratched over a window on the north side of the house are the initials and date, RS 1604. The Hall, now a farmhouse, can be approached by a public footpath from Heswall to Thurstaston church.

Gayton formed part of the original grant of land to Robert de Rodelent, at the time of the Conquest. After his death the lands were given by the Earl of Chester to another of his barons, Reginald de Tibermont. The Gleggs inherited the manor and estate of Gayton in 1330 and held them until 1758.

Gayton Hall is the traditional seat of the Gleggs. It was built in 1663 and is notable for a well-preserved columbarium (or pigeon breeding box). The outbuildings of the Hall were once protected by a moat and the situation, facing the Dee estuary, has given rise to a number of tales concerning smugglers amd maritime travellers.[36]

(vi) NESTON

In the early nineteenth-century the parish of Neston was the most populous in Wirral and consisted of eight townships: Great Neston, Little Neston, Leighton, Ness, Raby, Thornton Hough, Willaston and Ledsham. In 1086 part of the township of Great Neston was held by the monks of St. Werburgh under William Fitz-Nigel, baron of Halton. In the early twelfth-century William's son obtained the monks' portion in return for Raby. Shortly afterwards, the manor and church at Neston passed to Robert de Montalt.

In 1327 Neston passed to the king, Edward III, and in 1454 to the Earl of Salisbury. The manor was subsequently acquired by the sixth Earl of Derby (1598). In 1602 William Whitmore of Leighton obtained Neston from his father-in-law, Sir Hugh Beeston.

Neston may get its name from the natural headland which juts out into the estuary. In the eighteenth-century, Daniel Defoe described 'Nesson, a long nase or ness of land, which, running out into the sea, makes a kind of key.' Alternatively, the ness referred to might be Burton Point.

The earliest surviving plan of the township was drawn up for the Mostyn family (the Mostyns acquired a large portion of Neston in 1672) in 1732 and this indicates that the settlement followed a strip of sandstone outcrop that runs north to south. There was also the village's close proximity to a water supply: the stream that rises below Liverpool Road and flows out to the Old Quay site and the Dee.

Neston's eminence as a port and embarkation point, and later as a coaching post, declined with the silting of the Dee. There was a shift in shipping activities further north to Parkgate which by the early nineteenth-century had become a fashionable resort. However, until the mid-nineteenth century Neston remained the most populous place in Wirral with a weekly market and significant administrative status.

THE CHURCH OF ST. MARY AND ST. HELEN

Neston is one of five parishes in Wirral for which a priest is given in the Domesday book. The church was granted by Ralph, son of Robert de Montalt, to the Abbot and Convent of St. Werburgh sometime prior to 1182. It remained in the monks' possession until 1536 when it passed to the Dean and Chapter of Chester Cathedral.

There is a reference in the 1536 charter to the fact that the church had been rebuilt about 1150. Ormerod (1819) described 'a tower, nave, chancel, and side aisles, which seems originally to have terminated in private chancels.'[37] Prior to the 1875 restoration the nave was divided from the side aisle by 'four semi-circular arches on each side, resting on cylindrical columns with square capitals.'[38] These observations suggest that part of the Norman structure still existed in the nineteenth-century.

The rebuilding of the mediaeval church may have taken place before 1450; the tower was probably raised to its present height (the battlements were added in 1875) and the lower portion may contain pieces of Norman masonry. A weathered datestone on an angle buttress probably records some seventeenth-century renovation.

The top of each small window in the belfry chamber — facing south west — has been altered by the insertion of two square-shaped lintel stones. In the south window, this masonry is part of an old tombstone inscribed with a cross inside a circle. The inside stone in the west window has a carving of two men on horseback engaged in tilting.

In the mid seventeenth-century, the interior of the church was substantially altered. The chancel and nave were brought together by the demolition of the rood screen. The fourth Norman pillar, counting from the west, was removed together with the chapels, and the south wall of the church was rebuilt.

In the following century a 'hearse house' was built against the south wall of the tower and a vestry on the east end of the north aisle. In an attempt to provide more accommodation, galleries were erected and windows put in the chancel roof to provide more light. The Norman pillar at the west end of the south side was demolished to give the new gallery a better view of the three decker pulpit on the north side of the nave.

92.
Lintel stone in the belfry (Church of St. Mary and St. Helen, Neston).

Between 1711 and the late eighteenth-century, the two remaining arches in the chancel had been made into one. By 1775 the original Norman arch west of the church remained intact but the other four had been destroyed, replaced by two which were double the width of the original.

In 1874 the church was extensively rebuilt, and the work was finished in 1875. At this time, three stone fragments were discovered. The largest is carved with a figure of a priest, while another (which may have been part of the same pre-Norman cross) has on one side two men wrestling and on the other, a winged angel.

In 1986-8 the Neston Civic Society and the Parkgate Society embarked on a scheme to display the stones in conjunction with the Parish Council.

93.
Lower part of pre-Norman cross with interlacing, Neston.

94.
Mediaeval tombstone, Neston.

A mediaeval tombstone was also found, with a border of scrollwork and roses, and a number of small holes intended for coloured glass or jewels. All these pieces now remain within the church.[39]

The church fittings are mostly modern. In 1551 the vicar at Neston was ordered to surrender the greater part of his church ornaments.[40] The fifteenth-century octagonal font was turned out in the churchyard during the nineteenth-century restoration, but later replaced in the church.

The parish registers begin in 1559, although incomplete for the years 1674-1699. The early registers are actually late sixteenth-century parchment copies. The churchwardens' accounts start in 1701 and the list of rectors begins before 1182 with William de Montalt, vicars from 1307.

Chapter VI

Eastham and South Wirral

(i) EASTHAM

Nathaniel Hawthorne, the American author and Consul in Liverpool from 1853 to 1856, described Eastham as the finest old English village that he had seen 'with altogether a rural and picturesque aspect, utterly unlike anything in America.'[1] In the nineteenth-century Eastham Village was nicknamed 'the Richmond of Cheshire' owing to the fine woodland and splendid riverside views.

Although Eastham is now a Conservation Area, with a Country Park created in 1970, much damage had already been done to the landscape. In 1949 certain legal powers were transferred from the local District Council to the Manchester Ship Canal Company regarding industrial development in the area. After the second world war, the Queen Elizabeth II oil dock was constructed and Eastham was transformed into a village of storage tanks.

95.
Mediaeval spire (Church of St. Mary, Eastham).

The parish of Eastham formerly included the townships of Eastham, Childer Thornton, Hooton, Overpool, Netherpool, Great Sutton, Little Sutton and part of Whitby. In the Domesday Book the manor of Eastham, with its assessment of 22 hides, accounted for more than one fifth of the valuation of the whole hundred. In 1152 the church and manor house of Bromborough and Eastham were given by the third Earl of Chester to the Abbey of St. Werburgh.

After the Dissolution the lands were given to the new bishopric of Chester, and subsequently they passed to Sir Richard Cotton and Sir Rowland Stanley of Hooton. They remained in the Stanley family until 1847.

About one mile from the village, some 300 yards north of Eastham Ferry Hotel (1846) is the site of 'Job's Ferry,' originally established in 1509 by the Chester monks. The fourteen steps cut into the rock may mark the earliest known landing stage, although the name 'Job's Ferry' may date from the nineteenth-century.[2]

The original village inn stood opposite the Hooton Arms and was later moved to an old farm at the side of Eastham House (dated 1691 and now a home for the elderly).

The school, built in 1852, occupies the site of the old pound or pinfold. In the seventeenth century the parish school was at Childer Thornton.

THE CHURCH OF ST. MARY

The priest mentioned in the Domesday Book for Eastham, must have officiated at Bromborough. It is not until 1152 that Eastham and Bromborough appear in records as distinct manors with distinct churches. Before this time, Bromborough was the 'mother' church and Eastham merely a 'chapel.'

Although the outside of Eastham church is predominately Victorian, a little remains of the mediaeval structure. The early fourteenth-century broach spire was restored about 1752 and is one of only two in Wirral. The two side aisles are divided from the body of the church by four-bay arcades, of fourteenth-century origin.

96.
Stanley chapel. (Chapel of St. Mary, Eastham).

In the Stanley Chapel are two altar tombs to the memory of the Hooton Stanleys, dated 1612 and 1662. In the south aisle are three oak panels, now part of an organ screen, removed from the Poole's manorial pew in 1870. They are carved with heraldic devices, the arms of Poole, Poole quartered with Brereton(?) and Capenhurst, and have been called 'the most interesting specimens of old oak carving now remaining in Cheshire.'[3] They are probably early sixteenth-century work.

97.
Oak panels, (Church of St. Mary, Eastham).

In 1863 the whole of the south side of the chancel was almost completely rebuilt and restoration work in 1874 revealed 'bright scarlet lines...and other traces of decoration, probably dating from before the Reformation.'[4]

In 1876 the north wall of the church was rebuilt and the old brick vestry was removed. During the removal of the pews and flooring in the north aisle, the Norman foundations of the north wall were uncovered and the old north-west doorway revealed from the inside. The level of the floor was lowered to make these a feature.

The churchyard at Eastham is perhaps best known for the old yew tree which is of indeterminate age. The Royal Archaeological Society, who visited Eastham in 1898, thought it would have been planted against the east end window of the original (i.e. pre-Norman) church.

Alan Brack, during research for his book *The Wirral*, attempted to get the tree listed in *The Guinness Book of Records* as the oldest in Britain. In correspondence with a leading authority on tree-dating, it transpired that the Eastham yew could be more than 1,500 years old.[5]

The list of vicars at Eastham - their names are inscribed on the south wall of the church - begins in 1316 and the parish registers start in 1598.

(ii) HOOTON, NETHERPOOL AND LITTLE SUTTON

South of Eastham lies Hooton, which at the time of Domesday was held by Richard de Vernon. In 1410 the estate descended to a branch of the Stanley family. The old hall at Hooton occupied a site now covered by a large car park adjacent to Vauxhall Motors plant. It was a very imposing timber building, erected in 1488 and pulled down in 1778.

Another interesting building which has now disappeared is Pool Hall. This was demolished in 1937 to make way for paper mills. Norman Ellison remembered 'a pathetic, lonely relic, almost competely surrounded by the vast buildings of a modern factory.'[6]

Pool Hall was described by Mortimer (1847) as 'a remarkably fine specimen of the domestic architecture of (Henry VIII's) period' and 'one of the most interesting remains of which the county can boast.'[7] Built about 1540, the building may have been completed in 1574.[8] At Netherpool, in 1801, all thirteen inhabitants lived at this house.

The Poole family (sometimes Pulle, Pull or Polle) held considerable property in Cheshire, with lands in thirteen Wirral townships including Wallasey, Liscard, Woodchurch and Upton. They also held the office of steward of Birkenhead Priory at the Dissolution and other important positions such as high sheriff,

98.
Hooton Hall, from an engraving in Ormerod.

99.
Pool Hall. Courtesy Birkenhead Reference Library Collection.

justiciar and chamberlain at Chester. When Thomas Poole died in 1535 his property passed to the Talbots.[9]

In 1399 the Abbot of Chester was granted a licence by letters patent to fortify his manor house at Little Sutton, together with those at Saighton and Ince. This was sited about one quarter of a mile from Sutton Hall Farm. The old hall was taken down in the eighteenth-century and any architectural or historical evidence destroyed. The stones were reworked for the present farmhouse, and during construction work an ancient cemetery was discovered and possibly the remains of an ancient chapel.[10]

(iii) BURTON

The village of Burton has frequently been described as the prettiest in Wirral. The main street is certainly attractive, lined by old houses and cottages, but the new development is not far off. Burton was made a Conservation Area in 1974 when the Cheshire Planning Department noted: 'The small scale domestic architecture, much dating from the seventeenth-century, is built of a great variety of materials and includes some good and early examples of timber-framed houses.'

It is now fairly certain that the Burton mentioned in the Domesday Book is in Wirral rather than near Tarvin. An extent, or valuation survey, of 1296 made by the Bishop of Lichfield's officials lists seven villeins (tenants working on the lord's manor) which corresponds exactly to the Domesday description.[11] In the Middle Ages the manor and church of Burton belonged to the bishops of Coventry and Lichfield and remained in their possession until 1806.

Sometime before 1238 Burton church became 'prebendal' - that is the rector (appointed by the bishop of the diocese) would take the church revenues as his salary. Although an absentee, he would take a tenth of the produce of each parishioner each year, and the income of the glebe lands (those lands which were assigned to the Incumbent of a parish as part of the church's endowment). Part of the old tithebarn, where the produce of the parish was stored in the seventeenth-century, still exists off Puddington Lane (Barn Farm).

The church of Burton, and the tithes, were granted in 1238 by the Bishop of Coventry and Lichfield to the Hospital of St. Andrew in Denhall. The site of this hospital for the poor and shipwrecked, now a scheduled ancient monument, is about one mile west of Burton village and 160 yards south east of Denna Hall.

The masters of this institution were rectors of Burton until 1496 when they amalgamated with a similar foundation at Lichfield. After this time Burton church once again received a curate (or rector's assistant) at a salary of £30 a year.[12]

101.
Earthwork at Burton Point.

100.
Mediaeval coffin lid (Church of St.
Nicholas, Burton).

The church building was erected in 1721, although a small portion of the fourteenth-century structure remains at the eastern end of the north Massey chapel, with an Early English window. Further indications of an early church can be found in the porch, with a mediaeval coffin lid found during restoration work and now built up within the church wall, and two Norman capitals which were dug up in the churchyard.

Inside the church, the communion rails are early seventeenth-century and said to be the oldest in Wirral. In the north-east corner a glass case contains a first edition of John Foxe's *Book of Martyrs,* printed in London in 1562-3.

The parish registers start in 1538 and contain mixed entries, not always complete, until 1780.[13] The churchwardens' accounts begin in 1780.

At Burton Point, one mile south of the village, there are the remains of an earthwork; a single rampart with a ditch outside. This could be an Iron Age hill fort or perhaps more likely a Celtic fortification protecting a sheltered anchorage where men and supplies could be embarked.[14] The earthwork may have given rise to the place name, *burh-tun,* the farmstead by a fortified place. In 1875 some twenty nine skeletons were found near to this spot but it is not known whether these were the remains of a shipwrecked crew, or a battle.

The eighteenth-century ruin of Burton mill is situated near the top of the hill, to the north of the village. This probably replaced an earlier structure, for a mill at Burton is mentioned in a document of 1629. A mediaeval well, referred to in old documents as Patrick's Well and now called Hampston's Well after an old Burton family, has been renovated and restored as a recreation area. It lies below the village, off Station Road.

Our knowledge of Burton's past is greatly assisted by the researches of the local history society under the direction of Paul Booth from Liverpool University. This is one of the most active groups of its kind in Wirral, and the fruits of their labours are largely embodied in a history of the village to be published in 1984.[15]

116

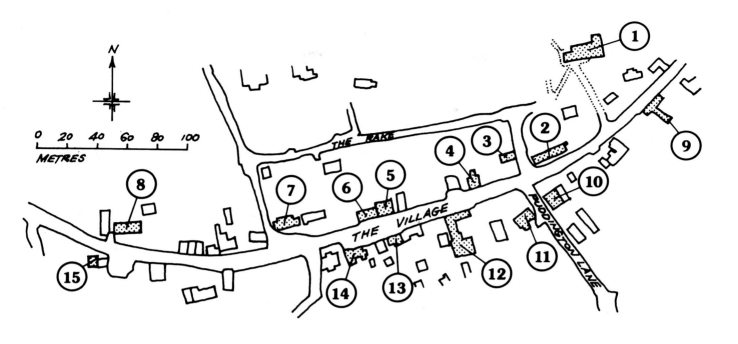

BURTON VILLAGE PRESENTS AN ASPECT OF TRADITIONAL ARCHITECTURE UNRIVALLED IN WIRRAL. MOST BUILDINGS DATE FROM THE 17TH. CENTURY, ALTHOUGH THE CHURCH OF ST. NICHOLAS (1) CONTAINS MEDIAEVAL WORK. ON THE NORTH SIDE OF THE VILLAGE THESE INCLUDE; SUNNY-BANK/PLESSINGTON COTTAGE (2), PEAR TREE COTTAGE (3), DATED 1682, ROSE COTTAGE (4) AND PICKERTON COTTAGE (5) AN ALTERED RED SANDSTONE STRUCTURE. STANLEY HOUSE (6) IS PARTLY TIMBER-FRAMED, WHILE BARN-END (7) IS SITED ON A SANDSTONE OUTCROP. BISHOP WILSONS COTTAGE (8) IS EARLY 17TH CENTURY IN ORIGIN, AND BIRTHPLACE OF THOMAS WILSON, BISHOP OF SODOR AND MAN. ON THE SOUTH SIDE OF THE VILLAGE, THE INTERIOR OF HILLSIDE/CHURCHVIEW (9) HAS OLD CHAMFERED BEAMS, THE WHITE HOUSE (12) CONTAINS AN ALTERED CRUCK STRUCTURE IN A BARN NEAR THE REAR ENTRANCE AND DELAMERE HOUSE (13) CONTAINS 14TH. CENTURY CRUCKS AT FIRST FLOOR LEVEL. THE HERMITAGE (14) AND GREENWOOD (15) ARE TIMBER FRAMED. IN PUDDINGTON LANE, CHURCH FARMHOUSE, CHURCH COTTAGE (10) IS C.1670 AND ELM FARMHOUSE (11) CONTAINS OLD DOORS AND CEILING BEAMS.

Fig. 12.
Burton's historic buildings. (Drawn by Alan Jones).

102.
The Village, Burton.

(iv) PUDDINGTON

The villages of Burton and Puddington come to mind when one talks of Wirral's attractive places. Although Puddington lacks the variety of traditional architecture found in Burton, the village is unspoilt and completely untarnished by modern development.

Mediaeval *Potitone* or *Pudyngton* was the original farmstead of the family of Pudds or Putta. In the eleventh-century it was held by Hamon de Mascy (Massey) and remained in the Massey family until 1716.

The Masseys of Puddington descended from Richard, a younger brother of Hamon, fifth baron. The sixth Hamon served at Poitiers (1356) while his son, Sir John Massey, was involved in the French wars of the late fourteenth-century. He was a knight of considerable reputation, sheriff of the county, and a lieutenant of North Wales. In 1398 he was granted a licence to build an oratory at his manor house of Puddington. Sir John died at the Battle of Shrewsbury in 1403.

103.
Puddington Old Hall.

Puddington Old Hall is an interesting survival of late mediaeval times. The roughcast exterior of the house looks quite ordinary, although inside the courtyard the partial remains of an oaken gallery are revealed. Internally, there are many old timbers and some old doors. The house was surrounded by a moat, and a drawbridge remained until the 1840's. Part of the moated enclosure still exists.

(v) SHOTWICK

If there is one Wirral village stuck in a time-warp, it is Shotwick. Situated at the end of a cul-de-sac, off the main Birkenhead to Queensferry road, time and the trappings of modern living have almost passed it by. In this respect, Shotwick is perhaps the most attractive, and certainly the least spoilt of Wirral villages.

Shotwick originally comprised five townships; Church and Rough Shotwick (or Woodbank), Great and Little Saughall, and Capenhurst. At the time of the Domesday survey, *Sotowicke* was held by the secular canons of St. Werburgh. A third part of the manor of Church Shotwick was subsequently granted to their successors, the Benedictine monks, by the first Earl of Chester. It remained with Chester Abbey and was leased to a local family until the reign of Edward I (1272-1307) when it passed to the Hockenhulls. They kept possession until 1715.[16]

The derivation of the place name is a matter for conjecture. The 'wick' may refer to ancient salt-works or the Scandinavian 'wik' for a creek. The 'shot' could refer to a personal name or a physical feature such as a spit or shot of land. Alternatively, the name may come from the Old Norse *sceot,* a steep slope, and *wic,* a hamlet.

In the Middle Ages Shotwick achieved great importance as a port and embarkation point at a time when the river lapped at the church walls. It also commanded an important crossing of the Dee and the ford was still in use in the early eighteenth-century. When the new straight channel of the Dee was constructed Shotwick Ford was abandoned. Chester Golf Club now occupies part of the reclaimed ground.

For many centuries the journey from Chester to Shotwick Ford was made along the 'Saltesway,' which also served the castle. This thoroughfare was supposedly used by Henry III in 1245, when he led a great army into Wales, and again in 1277 by Edward I. To the south of the church a cobbled lane, stretching toward Flint, may have been used as the regular route to Wales for travellers and military forces from Lancashire and Wirral.

104.
Church of St. Michael, Shotwick, from the south-west.

THE CHURCH OF ST. MICHAEL

The church at Shotwick has been called 'the only truly mediaeval church (in Wirral) to delight the senses.'[17] In mediaeval times it occupied a defensive position; to the west was the Dee estuary, to the north the moated and fortified site of the old hall, and to the south a tidal creek which now only exists as a small brook.

There is a mention in the parish registers for 1661 of a need for repairs to the church wall, after it had been demolished by the king's forces who were sheltering in the church. On the west wall of the porch are those deep indentations which could be arrow-head marks.

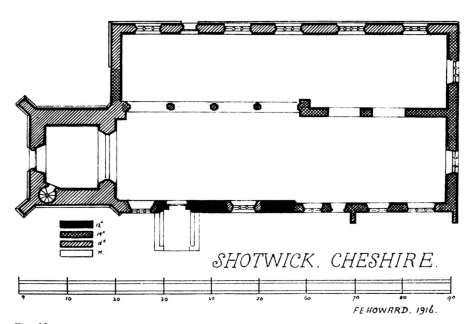

SHOTWICK. CHESHIRE.

F.E HOWARD. 1916.

Fig. 13.
Plan of Shotwick Church from F.H.Crossley, 'Cheshire Churches in the Twelfth Century', J.C.A.S., N.S., XXXII, Part II, (1938).

105.
Norman doorway, Shotwick.

The church is basically a twelfth-century structure with fourteenth-century alterations. It now consists of a south porch, nave, north aisle, a small chapel to the east (now housing the organ), a chancel, and an embattled west tower.

Of the early period there is a semi-circular doorway on the south side embellished with chevrons on a centre ring, flowers on the inner ring and three rows of billeting (short rectangular blocks). This is the only surviving example of a decorated Norman doorway in Wirral and it is somewhat obscured by a later porch. The south door is probably sixteenth-century.

In the fourteenth-century the church gained two aisles, with a chancel to the south and a chapel to the north. The chancel is divided from the chapel by two low arches resting on octagonal pillars. The north aisle and the main body of the church are separated by a range of four arches on decorated capitals. Part of the west end of the nave is fourteenth-century.

The twin-gabled east wall contains a three-light window with fragments of early sixteenth-century glass. The letters T.C. may refer to Thomas Clarke, the last Abbot of St. Werburgh who died in 1541. The 'Annunciation' group was only discovered in 1947.

The west tower has been called 'the attraction of this church.' It was probably built in the early sixteenth-century, on the evidence of masons' marks and a similarity to the towers at Wallasey, Bidston and Backford.[18]

The west face has a small Tudor doorway topped by a three-light window. There are three storeys divided by two strings. The lower string course features flower and animal ornamentation, the upper string gargoyles. On the south side, towards the top of the tower, are the letters TCMD, possibly another reference to Thomas Clarke and the year 1500.

106.
The nave, looking west (Church of St. Michael, Shotwick).

In 1549-50 Shotwick had one chalice and 'a range of iii belles.' The present chalice is dated 1685 and of the six bells two are dated 1616 and 1621. One bell, dated 1664, was found to be cracked and is now situated at the west end of the nave below the tower.[19]

Many of the church inscriptions have disappeared, possibly when the floors were reflagged in the early eighteenth-century. A flagstone in the chancel, within the altar rails, was for many years thought to commemorate Hockenhull the old squire of Shotwick, whose horse fell upon him. It is more likely that the inscription is not a bridle bit and two stirrups but I.C.C., for John Carter, a curate of Shotwick whose will was proved at Chester in 1587.[20]

107.
Flagstone in the chancel (Church of St. Michael, Shotwick).

The list of incumbents at Shotwick is incomplete. The registers date from 1681, with regular entries from 1698. From 1591 there are incomplete bishops' transcripts at Chester. The churchwardens' accounts begin in 1717.[21]

SHOTWICK PARK AND CASTLE

The royal manor of Shotwick probably included the whole of what is now known as Shotwick Park and also the greater part of Great Saughall. In 1278 Roger le Strange of Ellesmere was granted the manor and fishery of Castle Shotwick at a rent of nearly £20 a year. During his lordship a survey of the manor was carried out and the lands were valued at £18 16s. 10d.[22]

Shotwick Park was created in 1327 when it is likely that nearly all the land in the manor of Castle Shotwick was enclosed. The chamberlain of Chester was given the task of setting up the park out of the revenues of his office. Several entries in the chamberlain's accounts refer to the maintenance of the park which, at this time, was also known as Burnellswood, possibly after Robert Burnell a Bishop of Bath and Wells.[23] (At one time he held certain rights over Rough Shotwick and Saughall).

On 18 July 1351 William Stanley, the Master Forester of Wirral, was granted by privy seal the custody of the park with an annual fee of 30s.[24] By 1403 the park-keeper's salary was a penny a day and eight acres of land called Woodbank. The office of keeper, first mentioned in a grant of 1332, was obtained in 1430 by Sir William Troutbeck of Dunham who was the chamberlain of Chester. By 1452 it appears that the Troutbecks had gained the lease of Shotwick Park.

The importance of the Shotwick estate is reflected by the number of prominent people associated with the lease. In 1461, for example, the two manors of Shotwick and Great Saughall and the office of park-keeper was given to Eleanor, wife of Thomas Stanley. She was the daughter of the Earl of Salisbury and sister of Richard, Earl of Warwick (the 'Kingmaker').

In the early sixteenth-century the secretary and councillor to the Prince of Wales and clerk to the signet, Peter Merton, obtained the lease at a rent of £24 2s. 4d. In c.1512 Sir Ralph Egerton of Ridley was appointed Master of the Game at Shotwick but not park-keeper which was evidently a separate office. A contest then arose between the Brereton and Egerton families for the office of keeper. The Breretons gained the king's favour and in 1528 William Brereton and his brother gained the office for life. This arrangement did not last long for the Breretons were soon out of favour. William, senior, was beheaded in 1536 after his implication in the court scandal involving Ann Boleyn.[25]

In 1549 Richard Wilbraham was appointed park-keeper and four years later he gave up this grant in order to obtain a lease for sixty years of the demesne and manor of Shotwick, Great Saughall, the park-keeper's office, land in Woodbank and the fishery, at a rental of £24 3s. 4d. Richard was a member of another distinguished and wealthy family; he was Mary Tudor's Master of Revels and also in charge of her jewel house.

108.
Shotwick Castle.

To the north-west of Shotwick Park, south-west of Castle Farm, are two raised mounds which are all that remain of Shotwick Castle. It was probably built by the Normans in the late eleventh-century protecting an important ford of the Dee against the intrusions of the Welsh. In the thirteenth-century the castle was used by English kings but became less important after the death of the Welsh prince, Llywelyn, in 1282.

The castle is first mentioned in documents in 1240, and the fourteenth-century chamberlain's accounts record various repairs to the structure.[26] The ruins were noted as late as 1789 when the castle was described as a pentagon of fifty one feet on each side, with a watchtower five storeys high.[27]

In 1876 a local schoolmaster began preliminary excavation of the site, but no full account was published. According to Philip Sulley (1889) the foundations were revealed 'resting on great boulder pebbles, together with a pebbled roadway...Many pieces of glazed pottery of various periods was discovered...'[28]

SHOTWICK HALL

Shotwick Village possesses several seventeenth-century cottages and buildings, chief of which is the Hall which stands half a mile north of the church. The mediaeval manor house occupied a moated site in front of the present hall and traces of this moat are still visible.

In its present form, Shotwick-Hall dates from the mid seventeenth-century and it was the residence of the Hockenhull family until the 1730's. The entrance porch of the house opens to a large square hall, decorated with plaster work of flowers and animals. The interior has lost some of its historic and architectural features although a mantelpiece in the principal room bears the date 1662 and the Hockenhull coat of arms.

109.
Shotwick Hall.

(vi) BACKFORD

At the time of the Conquest, or soon afterwards, the manor and church of Backford was held by the barons of Dunham who made it part of the endowment of the priory at Birkenhead. At the Dissolution, the rectory and advowson of the church was transferred to the new bishopric of Chester.

The name of the village derives from *bach,* a stream, and *ford* a crossing place, although the term ford was also used to indicate a position on a Roman road. Backford had some importance as an administrative centre in the later Middle Ages. By the fourteenth-century it was the regular venue for the Eyre, a judicial court presided over by the justiciar of Chester.

THE CHURCH OF ST. OSWALD

The tower and a small part of the chancel are the only remains of the mediaeval church at Backford. The tower is early sixteenth-century, although the battlements are a modern addition, and it is probably the work of those masons responsible for the towers at Shotwick, Handley and Tattenhall. All are within a ten-mile radius of Chester. The chancel contains fourteenth-century work, and a fine three-light pointed east window. The remainder of the church was almost completely rebuilt in 1728.

The church is most interesting for its internal furnishings and fittings. It is, with Stoak, unique in containing a number of wooden monumental panels.[29] These were intended to be hung on the church walls as a permanent memorial to the deceased and, in this respect, they differed from *hatchments* which were wooden boards displayed in the house at the time of death and only occasionally transferred to a church for preservation. Each panel contains the arms and quarterings relating to a deceased person and their families, together with an inscription.

At least one of the Backford panels is the work of Randle Holme (1624-1704), a member of the famous Cheshire family who left behind a large and valuable collection of manuscripts relating to the county's history.[30]

110.
Wooden panel attributed to Randle Holme (Church of St. Oswald, Backford).

The Backford panel attributed to him, on the south wall next to the south entrance, is inscribed with the name of Lenox Beverley, who died in 1660, and Elizabeth, daughter of Henry Birkenhead of Backford, who died in 1656. The Birkenheads purchased the Backford estates in 1571, and resided at the old Backford Hall from about 1605.

To the left of this, another panel is dedicated to Elizabeth's younger sister and dated 1624. Also on the south wall are two tablets commemorating the Morgells of Moston. The earliest, above the font to the right, is dated 1627. To the right of the five-light window in the south wall, a panel records the death of Ralph Morgell of Moston who married Margaret, daughter of Edward Glegg of Gayton.

Randle Holme came into conflict with the London College of Heralds who claimed that he acted in the capacity of herald at funerals without legal authority. The Norroy King of Arms, Sir William Dugdale, then visited the churches where Holme's work was displayed in order to deface any offending panels. It seems that Dugdale failed to locate the Backford and Stoak works. Ultimately, Holme's ability was recognised and he was made deputy to the College of Arms for Chester, Lancashire and North Wales.

Of the remaining internal features of the church, there is one of Cheshire's few surviving aumbries. This 'wall cupboard' of the early sixteenth-century is placed near the altar in the south wall of the chancel. The plate, relics and vestments were placed here for safe keeping. Near to this, an ornamental bishop's chair is made from the original Jacobean oak altar rails.

The old oak parish chest was at one time hidden away in the vicar's potting shed, and the lid is made with old wood taken from Chester Cathedral. The chest is inscribed with the names of two churchwardens and the date 1636. Another interesting old relic is the old chained bible, printed in London in 1617, and now kept in a glass case in the nave.

The lists of vicars at Backford begins in 1305 with William de Aston and the parish registers start in 1562.

(vii) STOAK

In a not untypical turn of phrase, Ormerod described the village of Stoak as 'a collection of ragged and filthy hovels, scattered around the church without the least attention to arrangement.'[31] This famous Cheshire historian wrote in the early nineteenth-century, but the village prospect has not really changed much since then.

The earliest known lord of the manor is Roger de Soterleigh, before 1216, and the manor later passed to the Thorntons, the Duttons of Dutton and the Gerards of Fleetwood. Little Stanney, to the north of the parish, was the seat of the Bunburys of Bunbury who settled here in the twelfth-century. The old manor house, Stanney Hall, was pulled down in 1821.

THE CHURCH OF ST. LAWRENCE

In 1349 the church, and the manor of Stoak, was given by Peter de Thornton to the Dean and Chapter of St. John's church in Chester. In the fourteenth-century the living (or benefice) was leased to local families. After the Dissolution, the church passed to the Dean and Chapter of Chester Cathedral.

There was evidence of a twelfth-century structure before the church was extensively restored in 1827. Ormerod (1819) described a south doorway with chevron mouldings, concealed by a south porch, a blocked up north doorway and a carved font.[32] On the east end, a wooden transept projected to the south, and this was the early chapel of the Bunbury family. A drawing by Thomas Rickman, dated 1809 and now in the British Museum, shows the church from the south-east. It appears as a three chambered structure, each roof progressively lower in height toward the west.

In the restoration of 1827 the timber tower, the porch and south doorway, and the south side of the nave were destroyed. The chancel arch, the priest's doorway in the chancel, the timber Bunbury chapel and the west gallery and screen were also lost. The carved font may have been destroyed by workmen who lit a fire in it.

A new stone tower was then erected, the south side of the nave was rebuilt and a double transept was made out of the second chamber. The north wall of the nave, with a blocked up mediaeval doorway, and the basic Tudor chancel were left intact.

The church still retains the Tudor nave roof of four bays, of arch brace and hammer beam design. The roof timbers are original, with the addition of new rafters and plastering, and similar to those that existed at Stanney Hall.

Fragments of the old rood screen remain in the west gallery; eight pieces decorated with foliage and Gothic ornamentation which formed part of the wainscotting of the original screen.

The church at Stoak shares with Backford the distinction of wooden memorial boards. The Stoak collection has been described as the finest in the county and most are in memory of the Bunburys, forming a sort of geneaological history of this family from the late seventeenth-to the early nineteenth-century.

In the south transept, originally to the right of the window, there is a painted panel commemorating the death of Thomas Bunbury, the fourth son of Sir Henry Bunbury, who died in 1668. The frame is decorated with rosettes and crossbones, with cherubim at the corners. In the upper part of the frame, two shields are separated by the Bunbury crest. The shield on the left represents the marriage of

111.
The nave and arch-beam roof (Church of St. Lawrence, Stoak).

Thomas Bunbury to the only daughter of William Wilcocks. The shield to the right celebrates the marriage of Thomas to his second wife, Eleanor, the fifth daughter of Henry Birkenhead of Backford.

Another panel, at one time to the left of the window, records the death of Dulcibella in 1686. She was one of the daughters resulting from the marriage of Thomas to Eleanor and the panel features the arms of the Bunbury, Birkenhead and Norrey families.

112.
Wooden panel (Church of St. Lawrence, Stoak).

Of the other old church fittings, the altar rails and table are Jacobean and the church plate includes important early examples, notably an Elizabethan chalice now held by the Grosvenor Museum in Chester. The church bells are the oldest in Wirral, dated 1615, 1631 and 1642.[33] The parish registers are almost complete from 1543 while the extant churchwarden accounts start in 1677 but with many gaps.

Within the panel:
Anne daughter to Henry Bunbury esq
sone & heare of s^r Henry Bunbury K
dyed the 23th of september 1627.

113.
Wooden panel (Church of St. Lawrence, Stoak).

(viii) STANLOW ABBEY

Stanlow Point, now cut off from mainland Wirral by the Manchester Ship Canal, seems an unlikely spot for habitation. And yet centuries ago there was a monastery here, established in 1178 by John de Lacy, Constable of Chester and sixth baron of Halton. This bleak and isolated site seems plausible when one realises the austerity of the Cistercian Rule.

The monastery was endowed with the lands of Stanlow (mediaeval, *Stanlaw),* the township of Stanney, lands in Runcorn and a court house in Chester.[34] In the thirteenth-century it is clear that there was some rivalry between the monks of Stanlow and those of Chester over land and milling activities. An agreement was reached in 1209 which stated that the Stanlow monks had to find the Chester monks twenty-four cart loads of thatching at midsummer each year.

By the late thirteenth-century the sea was threatening this sacred site and actually damaged the church. In 1287 the tower collapsed. The brethren were obdurate. This was a place of pilgrimage and worship, the burial ground of the earls of Lincoln and the constables of Chester. They were not going to vacate their shrine so easily.

Two years later a fire swept away the greater part of the abbey. Ultimately, with their offices under three feet of water, the Stanlow monks petitioned Pope Nicholas IV and requested their migration to Whalley, some fifty miles away in Lancashire.

The transfer was not without drama. The monks of St. John at Pontefact claimed that they had rights to the benefice of Whalley, and claimed that the abbot there had been bribed by the monks of Stanlow. Henry de Lacy then intervened, and took forcible possession of the church at Whalley and retained it in return for the chapel of St. Mary in Clitheroe.

In January 1294 five of the monks and the Abbot remained at Stanlow, one went to Stanney grange, another to Oxford to complete his studies, and some twenty monks went to Whalley. Stanlow Abbey continued as a cell of five monks attached to Whalley Abbey until the Dissolution, when the lands passed to Sir Richard Cotton. An inventory of Stanlow Abbey's goods, made in 1537, lists a chapel, servants' and maidens' chambers, buttery, kitchen, brewhouse, courthouse and hall.[35]

The remains of the abbey site are now overgrown and inaccessible. In the nineteenth-century some of the old stones and columns were built up in the outbuildings of a farm. Ormerod mentions 'a small circular apartment' beneath the buildings which was probably a burial vault.

The site of the monks' grange is in Great Stanney, formerly part of the parish of Eastham. An artificial terrace called Grange Cow Worth is all that remained of the farmlands until early 1972 when a new housing estate smothered the area. Ormerod mentions 'traces of extensive buildings...occasionally laid bare by the plough...'[36] Excavations at the site in 1966 and 1967 (the present Ludlow and Rochester Drives) produced sherds of mediaeval pottery but the archaeologists stressed that their finds raised more questions than they answered.[37]

By the mid thirteenth-century, Stanlow Abbey actually had eight granges. This must have led to the employment of a local (i.e. non-clerical) peasantry. The grange, from earliest times, was a mixed farming community with little monastic interference.[38]

114.
Wall in the wilderness : remains of Stanlow Abbey.

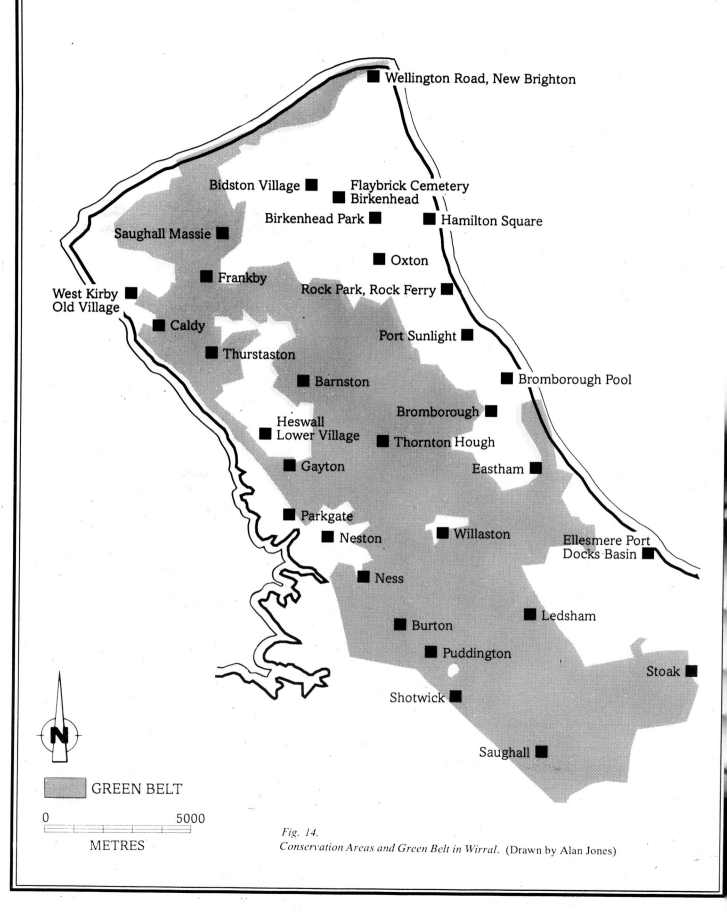

Conservation Areas and Green Belt in Wirral

Wellington Road, New Brighton

Bidston Village

Flaybrick Cemetery
Birkenhead

Birkenhead Park

Hamilton Square

Saughall Massie

Oxton

West Kirby
Old Village

Frankby

Rock Park, Rock Ferry

Caldy

Port Sunlight

Thurstaston

Barnston

Bromborough Pool

Heswall
Lower Village

Bromborough

Thornton Hough

Gayton

Eastham

Parkgate

Neston

Willaston

Ellesmere Port
Docks Basin

Ness

Ledsham

Burton

Puddington

Stoak

Shotwick

Saughall

N

GREEN BELT

0   5000

METRES

Fig. 14.
Conservation Areas and Green Belt in Wirral. (Drawn by Alan Jones)

Chapter VII

Preserving Wirral's Past

(i) PROTECTING THE COUNTRYSIDE: GREEN BELT POLICY

With the advent of the computer and micro-technology it is widely thought that leisure and recreation will be vitally important in future years, as people work less hours and have more time to spare. Ironically, unemployment in recent years has given people a greater opportunity to explore their immediate environment. All this, of course, is one reason to maintain part of Wirral as a recreational area and to preserve as much open space as possible. In simple terms, the countryside is a pleasant place to go to at weekends and the necessary 'lung' for an urban population. There is, though, more to it than this.

The landscape makes a fascinating study in itself. Field patterns, churches and earthworks combine to mould our countryside and our local heritage is a vital link with our ancestors. The historic buildings and villages provide a degree of stability and continuity in a changing world.[1]

The maintenance of Wirral's open spaces stems largely from *green belt* policies adopted by local councils. Although this land is valued for leisure purposes, its major function is agricultural. The green belt idea was first mooted in the 1920's. The establishment of a strip of open countryside around an urban area was the first step in reducing the development of open land for urban use and aimed at preserving the separate character of each town or village.

115.
Progress and the pastoral, Eastham.

In 1955 the government advised local planning authorities (i.e. county councils) to prepare green belts, and the Town and Country Planning Act of 1971 required the preparation of a 'structure plan' for each area.

Broadly speaking, the development of open land might be permitted in special circumstances but there would be an emphasis on the appearance of the surrounding area, and the facilities of the people living nearby. Planning permission within the green belt would normally only be granted for agriculture and leisure purposes.

The *Merseyside Green Belt Subject Plan* was published in 1981 and defined the precise boundaries of the open countryside in the Merseyside portion of Wirral.[2] In addition, it outlined the council's policy in determining planning applications in and adjacent to the green belt. Certain areas were designated 'heritage landscapes,' such as the Dee coastline and Thornton Hough, and local nature reserves were proposed at Hilbre and Thurstaston.

The first green belt proposals by Cheshire County Council were submitted in 1961. A series of provisional documents have outlined the council's policy for rural Cheshire.[3] In 1972 it was stated that areas of special (landscape) value would be designated in the local plans and in these areas no housing, industrial or commercial development would be allowed. In 1976 the County Structure Plan aimed to define more clearly those parts of rural Cheshire worthy of special protection. In Wirral, the Neston-Parkgate coast was mentioned.

The green belt proposals for the Cheshire part of Wirral are still only provisional although the original boundaries have generally been maintained. Since local government reorganisation in 1974 most detailed planning decisions are taken by the district councils. Each council has to set up a Local Plan and that for Ellesmere Port and Neston is still in progress.

(ii) CONSERVATION AREAS

The origins of the conservation area go back at least to the 1930's when, in 1931, the Ancient Monuments Act established the principle of protecting a whole area rather than a particular building. Under the provisions of the 1967 Civic Amenities Act local councils were required to designate 'conservation areas' of special architectural or historic interest. More publicity was to be given about planning applications and proposals to alter or demolish buildings.

Once an area is designated, the local council has wide ranging powers of control. Under the Town and Country Planning Act of 1968, for example, the council can serve a Repairs Notice on an owner who is allowing a listed building to deteriorate beyond repair, thus affecting the character of a conservation area.

Both Wirral Borough and Cheshire County Council have adopted the 'three stage' planning approach to conservation. Stage 1 entails the designation of an area, Stage 2 involves the formulation of detailed policies and improvement schemes and Stage 3 sees the execution of these policies.[4] Many proposals will only reach Stage 2 as a result of financial constraints and economic recession.

BIDSTON

Bidston Village was finally made a conservation area in 1972 by the Borough Council of Birkenhead. In 1976 Wirral Borough Council reassessed the problems facing this historic village. By this time, many buildings had deteriorated and the appearance of the village had declined.

It was proposed that 'new' but 'sensitively designed' housing could be erected between the existing properties south of Bidston Village Road in order to provide 'continuity of street scene.'[5] New development and 'link' buildings, rather than a restriction, was seen as the answer to Bidston's problems.

A further report on Bidston was produced in February 1983 and a significant reorientation of the village was noticed. The presence of livery stables - a horse-based economy - had re-established Bidston as a rural village, and helped to pay for the upkeep of the historic buildings.[6]

It was thought that the best way to preserve Bidston's unique character was to discourage development on the south side of Bidston Village Road. The north side, however, had problems due to the lack of investment. The building known as 'The Lilacs,' for example, had been derelict for some years.

In summary, the main problem besetting Bidston is traffic; the village remains the exit road of the Ford housing estate. The council has considered that no practical or financial means would achieve a reduction of traffic flow.

116.
'The Lilacs', Bidston, c.1910. Courtesy Birkenhead Reference Library Collection.

117.
'The Lilacs', Bidston in 1983.

WILLASTON

Willaston is frequently quoted as one of the best examples of how progress can be allied to the past. A typical English village atmosphere remains in the centre.

In 1966 Willaston was the first Wirral village to be subject to a detailed conservation plan and three years later a Stage 1 report was published. This led to the designation of the central part of the village as a conservation area.

In 1971 a Stage 2 report proposed detailed schemes for the village and suggested policies to stimulate local discussion.[7] The report outlined the way Willaston changed from an agriculturally and architecturally distinct village, with a nucleus of buildings grouped around a village green, to a primarily residential settlement as a result of industry, personal transport and population expansion.

One of the basic elements of this plan was to take traffic away from the village square. Four sites were noted as vital to the future of the conservation area; Old

Hall Farm, Smithy Cottages, Ash Tree Farm and Cherry Brow Farm. The cost to improve Willaston's environment was estimated at £110,000, to be shared amongst the county and urban district council and private developers and individuals.

The basic tenets of this report have not been fully implemented. For example, traffic has not been removed from the village centre and in 1983 the Smithy Cottages site remains undeveloped.

One noticeable feature of Willaston's recent conservation history is the great community spirit which has been harnessed to improve and rejuvenate the village. In 1970 there was strong criticism from both visitors and locals that Willaston was shabby and neglected. In August of that year a sign mysteriously appeared on the green proclaiming 'The Worst Kept Village.' This acted as a catalyst and there was immediate response from local residents. An 'action committee' was formed and, with the help of scouts, schools and women's organisations, roads and houses were tidied up.

This new-found local awareness and pride in heritage reached a climax in 1975 - designated European Architectural Heritage Year - when Willaston celebrated the first of its Festivals centred around the village green.

(iii) PROTECTING THE BUILDINGS: PRESERVATION AND RESTORATION

The preservation of old buildings is a tightrope walk between preservation for aesthetic or architectural reasons, and demolition or modification due to advanced decay. In his foreword to the late Max Faulkner's *'Appeal for Survival'* Alan Brack wrote: 'All that is old should not be preserved merely because it is old. It is when it is old and pleasing to the eye that we ought to take all possible steps to preserve it.'[8] To some extent this is true, but many Wirral buildings - not necessarily 'pleasing to the eye' but fascinating for architectural detail and historic associations - have been lost or radically altered to conform with differing tastes and trends.

Irby Hall, for example, was a fine example of a half-timbered late sixteenth century manor house. It was radically restored in the late nineteenth-century and all interior, and many exterior, features were lost. In the 1970s a previous owner effected more changes which included the loss of a chimney. 'Mother Redcap's' in Wallasey was an eyesore, when it was demolished in 1974, but the building held so many local memories. The site still remains undeveloped.

Margaret Wood in her important book on *The English Mediaeval House* puts the case for preservation most succinctly, although indirectly.

> 'The charm of mediaeval architecture lies not in its intrinsic beauty alone...It is a link with our ancestors...The essence of the past still lingers like notes of distant music...and for a while our spirits are in tune.'[9]

Town and Country Planning legislation provides a framework for each local council to preserve buildings or groups of buildings. In 1932 an Act allowed local councils to make a preservation order in respect of any building of special architectural or historic interest in their area.

The 1944 Act introduced the statutory listing of historic buildings, whether inhabited or not, and three years later came the three listing categories.

> Grade 1 covered those buildings of outstanding interest, normally applied to large country houses.
> Grade 2 covered those buildings of special interest worthy of preservation (a Grade 2* listing was later introduced to mark particularly important buildings within the Grade 2 category).
> Grade 3 covered those buildings which although not outstanding contributed to the special character of an area. This category was abolished in 1969 although the Town and Country Planning Act of 1971 afforded further protection to this type of building.

Buildings might be listed for architecture, style or historic associations after a survey carried out by a Department of Environment inspector. 'Listed buildings consent' must be sought for any proposal to demolish or alter a building categorised in this way.[10]

RESTORATION

The owners of historic houses face potential problems of age; crumbling stonework, rotting timbers, and subsidence. In 1978, for example, there was a fight to save the eighteenth–century Cherry Brow Farm, in Hadlow Road, Willaston. The owner, a Heswall builder, claimed that the farmhouse was beyond repair and should be pulled down: 'The building is getting like an old suit. Once you patch one leg the other one goes. There comes a time in the life of a brick when every time you bang them together they just go again.'[11]

Improvement grants are available under the Housing Acts for basic amenities, from the local council. Under the historic buildings legislation, the county or district council can make grants or loans for the repair and maintenance of all listed buildings and for those buildings which although not listed are of architectural or historic interest. Further funds might be made available from the Historic Buildings Council and the Civic Trust but usually only for important buildings and those which have a 'group value' in a conservation area.

ASH TREE FARM AND THE OLD RED LION, WILLASTON

In 1967 an application was made to develop the site of Ash Tree Farm for housing, and it looked as if the farmhouse would be demolished and the farm outbuildings would make way for road widening. In 1969 the house was sold to local architect Bill Hardman who set about preserving the structure in very much its original state.

Restoration involved the renovation of sandstone features on the north wing and the stripping of the roof. Ash Tree Farm was something of a 'test case' in the late-1960s, and Bill Hardman proved that it was possible to retain the essence of a historic building in an advanced state of decay.

118.
Ash Tree Farm, Willaston, before restoration. Courtesy Birkenhead Reference Library Collection.

The Old Red Lion is possibly the best known of Willaston's old buildings. In 1962 an application to demolish the building and erect a new public house was turned down by the local council and a preservation order was served on the building in 1964.

This building does, however, furnish an example of a restoration project that somehow went hopelessly wrong. To the visitor it may appear as the archetypal Elizabethan edifice. Bill Hardman was involved in overseeing the restoration plans until planning permission was granted, but he was horrified by their

135

east elevation

north elevation

section

ground floor plan

⅛ inch to 1 foot

Fig. 15.
Plans of the Old Red Lion, Willaston, (a) prior to restoration from Cheshire County Council,
Willaston Stage 2 Conservation Report, (Chester, 1971) and (b) Bill Hardman's original
survey c.1972.

136

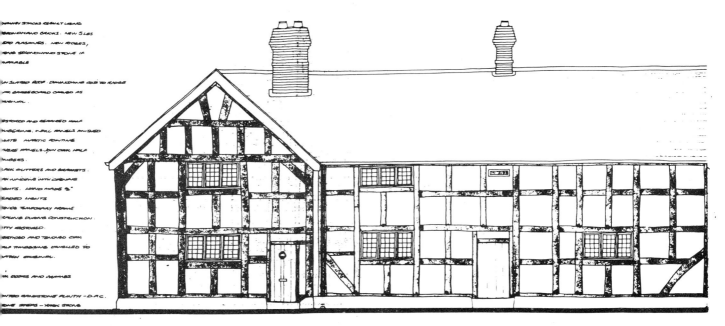

CHIMNEY STACKS REBUILT USING
SECONDHAND BRICKS. NEW SLABS
AND FLASHINGS. NEW RIDGES,
USING SECONDHAND STONE IF
AVAILABLE

NEW SLATED ROOF. DIMINISHING COS. TO RIDGE
NEW BARGEBOARD CARVED AS
ORIGINAL.

RESTORED AND REPAIRED HALF
TIMBERING. WALL PANELS PAINTED
WHITE. MASTIC POINTING
THESE PANELS JOIN OAK HALF
TIMBERS.

OAK GUTTERS AND BRACKETS.
NEW WINDOWS WITH OPENING
LIGHTS, HAND MADE ½"
LEADED LIGHTS
REMOVE TEMPORARY HOUSE
OPENING DURING CONSTRUCTION.
TOTTY RESTORED.
RESTORED AND TENONED OAK
HALF TIMBERING DOWELLED TO
MATCH ORIGINAL.

OAK DOORS AND FRAMES.

PAINTED SANDSTONE PLINTH - D.P.C.
STONE STEPS - YORK STONE

ELEVATION TO GREEN

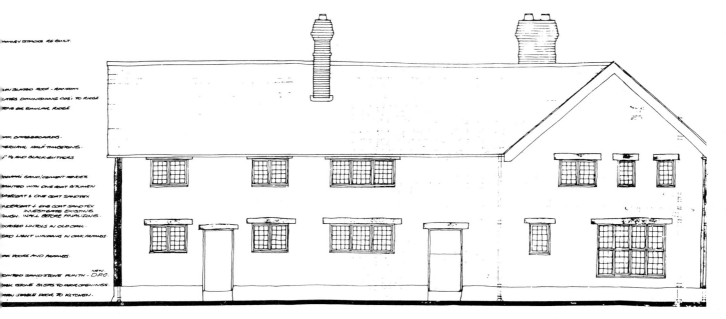

CHIMNEY STACKS RE-BUILT.

NEW SLATED ROOF - RANDOM
SLATES DIMINISHING COS. TO RIDGE
STONE OR SIMILAR RIDGE

OAK BARGEBOARDS.
INTERNALL HALF TIMBERING.
5" ½ AND BLACK GUTTERS

MODERN SAND/CEMENT RENDER
PAINTED WITH ONE COAT BITUMEN
BASECOAT & ONE COAT SANDTEX
BASECOAT & ONE COAT SANDTEX
INVESTIGATE EXISTING
FINISH. WALL BEFORE FINALIZING.
EXPOSED LINTOLS IN OLD OAK.
LEAD LIGHT WINDOWS IN OAK FRAMES.

OAK DOORS AND FRAMES.

PAINTED SAND STONE PLINTH - D.P.C. NEW.
DARK STONE STEPS TO ALL OPENINGS.
NEW STABLE DOOR TO KITCHEN.

ELEVATION TO GARDEN

1:48   RESTORATION OF THE OLD RED LION WILLASTON

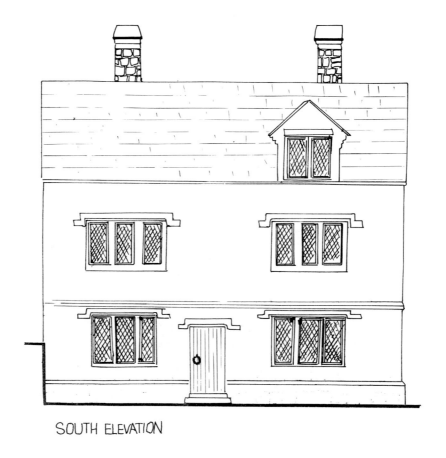

SOUTH ELEVATION

WEST ELEVATION

Fig. 16.
Plans for the restoration of the Old Rectory, Wallasey.

138

NORTH ELEVATION

EAST ELEVATION

PROPOSED RENOVATION and EXTENSION of THE OLD RECTORY, CHURCH HILL, WALLASEY, MERSEYSIDE

ELIZABETH and VAUGHAN LANCASTER-THOMAS

1:50 elevations

date: 1st August 1982
(amendments)

139

119.
Interior of the Old Rectory, Wallasey, before restoration.

execution. In his opinion, the finished result is 'basically an old fashioned building that's been built in the 1970s.'

The restoration involved the virtual demolition of the structure and its re-erection. There was, though, no real need for this.

THE OLD RECTORY, WALLASEY

The sandstone building beneath the church at Wallasey stood for many years exposed to the elements. In the summer of 1981 the old rectory was bought by Elizabeth and Vaughan Lancaster-Thomas who aimed to recreate the building in its original state using traditional methods and materials.

During restoration work a well was uncovered which may have served the original cottage. This well will be a central feature of the restoration plans and the couple hope that eventually local residents will visit the house and re-live a small, but important piece of Wallasey's past.

(iii) THE FUTURE FOR WIRRAL'S PAST

In January 1982 the Director of Leisure Services for Wirral Borough Council outlined the potential of Wirral as a tourist attraction and in 1983 the area was promoted as 'a pleasant place to go...and stay.' In his report, Brian Barnes drew attention to the countryside, the natural beauty, the historic buildings and the country parks.

In a sense, Wirral pioneered the idea of a country park when a group of Wirral residents prepared a report suggesting a linear recreation area based on the route of the old West Kirby to Hooton railway. The passing of the Countryside Act in 1968 gave the idea some incentive, and the Wirral Country Park was among the first projects to be recommended by the Countryside Commission. It was officially opened in October 1973 and is now one of Wirral's most popular recreational amenities.

Eastham Woods was designated a country park in 1970 as a contribution to European Conservation Year. A North Wirral Coastal Park was first discussed by the Wirral Green Belt Council in late-1972, with the idea of linking the Wirral Country Park at West Kirby with the Wallasey coast. The preliminary report suggested the use of Leasowe Castle, and the lighthouse, as an integral part of the park.

Although the idea of a country park is fairly well established in Wirral, that of a heritage park is not. In his report to the council in 1982, the Director of Leisure Services suggested that a Wirral Heritage Centre might bring together local history collections and archives and make them available for study.

Later that year ambitious plans for a 'Monk's Ferry Heritage Park' at the Birkenhead Priory site were discussed, and it was proposed that this would incorporate a 'heritage centre' and shipbuilding museum.

The Priory is unusual in that it is the only historic site in Wirral administered by a local council. Most of Wirral's historic buildings are in the custody of private owners or tenants and as a result of this they are inaccessible to the public. There are, happily, one or two exceptions. Leasowe Castle in Wallasey is now a hotel-cum-caravan centre, and Corner House Farm in Willaston has become a restaurant. Dawn Mallinson has opened the old vaulted chamber at the base of Brimstage Tower for light meals and teas and at Poulton Hall June Lancelyn Green is developing the garden's potential and an open day was held in June 1983 under the National Gardens Scheme. The owners and tenants of Wirral's historic houses do not face the financial problems of a Longleat or Chatsworth but it is noticeable that some are looking towards profitable enterprise and exploiting their immediate surroundings.

It would seem that Wirral has much to offer in terms of open countryside but even with green belt policies and conservation areas there is no room for complacency. The Council for the Protection of Rural England (CPRE) claimed, in 1982, that government planning policies favoured developers at the expense of widely accepted policies of restraint.[12] It warned that there was a very real prospect of villages merging with each other with both housing and industrial developers destroying open land.

In 1983 the CPRE warned that, in the climate of economic recession and unemployment, pressure on land was greater than at any time since the thirties and that the government might be prepared to sacrifice land in an attempt to buy jobs.

In Wirral, Ellesmere Port and Neston Borough Council have been heavily criticised for proposals to turn over green belt land in south Wirral for industrial purposes. It is argued that this contradicts the national policy for urban regeneration; the idea that derelict and unused land in towns should receive priority for development.

120.
Wirral landscape, near Neston.

There were fears, too, about the so-called 'M53 corridor' after the publication in 1981 of the *Merseyside Green Belt Subject Plan.* This 'corridor' separating Bidston from Upton and Moreton, was actually deleted from the council's revised proposals published in 1983.

All this means that, even bearing in mind conservation policies and legislation, we cannot be sure that our countryside and historic buildings will remain intact. Wirral is fortunate in having several long-established 'action' groups who closely guard our heritage and monitor the machinations of council planners and private developers.[13]

The Wirral Society was founded in 1928 and is affiliated to the CPRE. It aims to save the heritage of Wirral for the benefit of future generations and preserve the special character of the peninsula. The executive committee act as a watchdog, and consider planning applications which might affect the green belt and any threats to historic buildings.

During its long history, the society has had several notable 'victories' including the preservation of Willaston Mill and the Old Red Lion and, with The Bromborough Society, Stanhope House. The Wirral Society is itself affiliated to the Wirral Green Belt Council, a body composed of representatives of some 40 organisations, all having a positive interest in Wirral's preservation for present and future generations.

The future for Wirral's heritage is very much a matter for spirited co-operation - between authorities, developers, interested individuals and the public. Conservation should not be an isolated business but should complement modern living and historic buildings should not be preserved merely as museum pieces but become an integral part of the local community.

Perhaps most important, the people of Wirral should be made aware of their historic surroundings. A greater appreciation and understanding of our heritage - the lives of our ancestors, their places of work, worship and rest - can only enhance and sustain our own lives in the future.

Fig. 17.
Wirral Country Park at Willaston. (Drawn by Shirley Robinson).

NOTES

The following abbreviations are used in the references to the text. In the case of the Historic Society Transactions, the year of each volume given is not that of publication.

The place of publication, for all references, is London unless otherwise stated.

Chet. Soc.   Chetham Society (Manchester).

J.C.A.S.   Journal of the Chester Archaeological Society (Chester). Prior to Vol.54 (1967) the publication was known as the Journal of the Chester and North Wales Architectural, Archaeological, and Historic Society.

J.M.A.S.   Journal of the Merseyside Archaeological Society (Liverpool University).

Mortimer   W.W.Mortimer, *The History of the Hundred of Wirral with a Sketch of the City and County of Chester* (1847, republished Manchester, 1976).

Ormerod   G.Ormerod, *The History of the County Palatine and City of Chester*, Vol.2, (1819), 2nd Edition, revised and enlarged by T.Helsby (1882).

Rec. Soc.   The Record Society of Lancashire and Cheshire (Lancashire).

Sulley   P.Sulley, *The Hundred of Wirral* (Birkenhead, 1889).

T.H.S.L.C.   Transactions of the Historic Society of Lancashire and Cheshire (Lancashire).

T.L.C.A.S.   Transactions of the Lancashire and Cheshire Antiquarian Society (Lancashire).

V.C.H.   *Victoria County History of Chester* (ed. B.E.Harris), Vol.2, (1979), Vol.3, (1980).

W.N. & Q.   *Wirral Notes and Queries* (ed. F.Sanders and W.F.Irvine), Vol.1 (Birkenhead, 1892), Vol.2 (Birkenhead, 1893).

Chapter 1: An Introduction to Wirral

1   I owe this point to Dr. G.Lloyd-Morgan of The Grosvenor Museum, Chester. See G.D.B.Jones, 'The Romans in the North West', *Northern History*, III, (Leeds University, 1968) p.2.

2   See G.E.Connah, 'Roman Wirral — An Index of the Archaeological Evidence' in *The Bromborough Society 27th Annual Report* (1959-1960), pp.14-24. C.E.Thornton, 'Roman Discoveries in Wirral', *The Wirral Journal*, Vol.1, No.4, (Upton, 1982) pp.4-7.

3   G.Chitty, 'Wirral Rural Fringes Survey', *J.M.A.S.*, Volume 2, (1978) p.4.

4   See Chapter V, p.103.

5   Thornton, *op. cit.*, pp. 6-7.
A Roman pottery bowl was discovered during the Second World War at a house in Mill Hill Road, Irby. In 1989 Liverpool Museum excavated a short section across a ditch revealed during building work at the same site. Several Roman pottery sherds were discovered.

Further excavations carried out in April and May 1991 revealed food fragments, small lumps of coal and the remains of a handmill. Field Archaeologist Rob Philpott concluded that it was the site of a simple isolated farmstead. See R.A. Philpott, 'The Romans In Wirral', *The Wirral Journal*, Vol.5, No.7 (Upton, 1991) pp.27-29. 'Recent archaeological work on a Romano-British farmstead in Irby', *The Wirral Journal*, Vol.6, No.6 (Upton, 1993) pp.42-44. 'Merseyside In The Roman Period', in *J.M.A.S.*, Volume 7 (1991), pp.61-74.

6   For example, see W.F.Irvine in *Cheshire Sheaf*, Volume 44, (Chester, 1957) p.25 (No. 10242) et. seq. S.O'Dwyer, *The Roman Roads of Cheshire* (Newtown, 1935). I.D.Margary, *Roman Roads in Britain* (1955) pp.299-300. K.E.Jermy, 'The Roman Road in Wirral', *J.C.A.S.*, Vol.48, (1961) pp.1-13.

7   Jermy, *op. cit.*, See also, 'Fieldwork on the Roman Road at Street Hey, Willaston', in *The Bromborough Society 28th Annual Report* (1960-1961), pp.14-16.
Further excavations in 1962 revealed a line of kerbstones immediately east of Hargrave Lane, and in the field bounded on the north by the B5133 road and on the west by Heath Lane. See Jermy, 'The Roman Road in Wirral Air Photography and some Further Notes', *J.C.A.S.*, Vol.50, (1963) pp.1-2.

8   W.H.Massie, 'On a wooden bridge, found buried fourteen feet deep under the silt at Birkenhead', *J.C.A.S.*, Vol.1, (1850) pp.55-60; pp.68-76.
W.T.Watkin, *Roman Cheshire* (Liverpool, 1886; reprint with introduction by D.F. Petch, Wakefield, 1974) pp.80-82.

9   P. France, 'Roman Roads in Wirral', *The Wirral Journal*, Vol.3, No.1, (Upton, 1986) pp.30-33 and *The Wirral Journal*, Vol.3, No.2, (Upton, 1986) pp.14-18.

10   *Sulley*, p.117

11   Watkin, *op. cit.*, p.58.

12   This is, of course, very much simplified. I am not saying here that we should accept the Gildas account without reservation, but the general outline has proved tenable. See M.Winterbottom (ed.), *Gildas* (Phillimore Arthurian Period Sources Vol.7, Chichester, 1978).
L.Alcock, *Arthur's Britain* (1971) pp.21-44. L. & J. Laing, *Anglo-Saxon England* (1982) pp.41-49. J.D.Bu'Lock, *Pre-Conquest Cheshire 383-1066* (Chester, 1972) pp.9-20. J.McN. Dodgson, 'The English Arrival in Cheshire', *T.H.S.L.C.*, Vol.119, (1967) pp.1-37.

13   Bede, *A History of the English Church and People* Translated by L.Sherley-Price, (Revised edition, Harmonsworth, 1968) p.56.

14   D.Sylvester, 'Cheshire in the Dark Ages', *T.H.S.L.C.*, Vol.114, (1962) pp.1-22. The standard work on place-names is J.McN.Dodgson, *The Place-Names of Cheshire*, Part IV, (English Place-Name Society, Vol.XLVII, Cambridge, 1972). See also, W.F.Irvine, 'Place-Names in the Hundred of Wirral', *T.H.S.L.C.*, N.S., II & III, (1891-2), pp.279-304. G.Barnes, 'The Evidence of Place-Names for the Scandinavian Settlements in Cheshire', *T.L.C.A.S.*, Vol.LXIII, (1952-3) pp.131-155.

15   For the discovery of the stone see the description by G.F.Browne, 'On a Sculptured Stone with a Runic Inscription in Cheshire', *J.C.A.S.*, N.S., III, (1890) pp.178-184 and W.Dallow, 'Notes on the Overchurch Runic Stone', *op. cit.*, pp.185-191. See also, E.W.Cox, 'Overchurch and its Runic Stone', *T.H.S.L.C.*, N.S., II & III, (1891-2), pp.305-20.

16   This was the underlying theme of the exhibition, *The Vikings in England*, staged at The Yorkshire Museum, York in 1982.

17   F.T.Wainwright, 'Ingimund's Invasion', *English Historical Review*, LXIII, (1948), pp.145-169. See also, Wainwright, 'North-West Mercia A.D. 871-924', *T.H.S.L.C.*, Vol.94, (1942) pp.3-55.

18   F.T. Wainwright, 'North-West Mercia A.D. 871-924', T.H.S.L.C., Vol. 94, (1942) p. 48. The commercial role of Meols at this time is discussed in D. Griffiths, 'The Coastal Trading Ports of the Irish Sea', in J. Graham-Campbell (ed.) *Viking Treasure from the North West* : The *Cuerdale Hoard in its Context*, Liverpool Museum Occasional Paper No.5 (Liverpool, 1992) pp.67-69.

19   See R.N.Bailey, *Viking Age Sculpture in Northern England* (1980).

20   J.D.Bu'Lock, 'Pre-Norman Crosses of West Cheshire', *T.L.C.A.S.*, LXVIII, (1958) pp.1-9. J.R.Allen, 'The Early Christian Monuments of Lancashire and Cheshire', *T.H.S.L.C.*, N.S.,IX, (1893) pp.1-32.

21   See R.Stewart-Brown, *The Wapentake of Wirral* (Liverpool, 1951).

22   An excellent modern edition of the Domesday survey is featured in Phillimore's *'History from the Sources'* series : P.Morgan (ed.) *Domesday Book*, Vol.26 (Cheshire), (Chichester, 1978). See also, J.Tait (ed.), *The Domesday Survey of Cheshire*, *Chet. Soc.*, 2nd Series, Vol.75 (1916). J.Brownbill, 'Cheshire in the Domesday Book', *T.H.S.L.C.*, N.S., XV, (1901) pp.1-26. W.F.Irvine, 'Notes on the Domesday Survey, so far as it relates to the Hundred of Wirral', *J.C.A.S.*, V (1893) pp.72-84. I.B.Terrett, 'Cheshire', in H.C.Darby and I.S.Maxwell (ed.) *The Domesday Geography of Northern England* (Cambridge, 1962) pp.330-391. B.M.C.Husain, *Cheshire Under the Norman Earls, 1066-1237* (Chester 1973) pp.30-34.

23   See D.Sylvester, 'Cheshire Woodland in the Middle Ages', *The Cheshire Historian*, No.7, (Chester, 1957). I.B.Terrett, 'The Domesday Woodland of Cheshire', *T.H.S.L.C.*, Vol.100, (1948) pp.1-7.

24   R.N.Jones and P.H.W.Booth, 'Burton-in-Wirral : From Domesday to Dormitory', *Cheshire History Newsletter*, No.11, (Chester, 1976) pp.15-20.

25 See below, p.31.
J.Brownbill, 'Ancient Church Dedications in Cheshire and South Lancashire', *T.H.S.L.C.*, N.S., XVIII, (1902) pp.19-44. For a list of pre-Domesday parishes see J.D.Bu'Lock, *Pre-Conquest Cheshire 383-1066* (Chester, 1972) pp.78-9.

26 G.Barraclough, 'The Earldom and County Palatine of Chester', *T.H.S.L.C.*, Vol.103, (1951) pp.23-57. For alternative view, see H.J.Hewitt, *Mediaeval Cheshire*, Chet. Soc. 2nd series, Vol.88, (1929).

27 R.R.Davies, 'Richard II and the Principality of Chester', in *The Reign of Richard II : Essays in Honour of May McKisack* (ed.) F.R.H.Du Boulay and C.M.Barron, (1971) pp.256-79.

28 See P.H.W.Booth, 'Taxation and Public Order : Cheshire in 1353', *Northern History*, XII, (Leeds University, 1976) pp.16-31.
For financial administration in the fourteenth century, see P.H.W.Booth, *The Financial Administration of the Lordship and County of Chester, 1272-1377*, Chet. Soc., 3rd Series, Vol.28, (1981). R.Stewart-Brown (ed.) *Accounts of the Chamberlains and other Officers of the County of Chester 1301-1360, Rec. Soc.*, LIX, (1910).

29 R.Stewart-Brown, *The Serjeants of the Peace in Medieval England and Wales* (1936).

30 See below, pp.27-28.

31 See R.Stewart-Brown, 'The Disafforestation of Wirral', *T.H.S.L.C.*, N.S., XXIII, (1907) pp.165-180 'Further notes on the Disafforestation of Wirral', *T.H.S.L.C.*, Vol.89, (1937) pp.23-27. 'The Charter and Horn of the Master-Forester of Wirral', *T.H.S.L.C.*, Vol.87, (1935) pp.97-112.

32 See J.C.Cox, *The Royal Forests of England* (1905) pp.10-24. J.D.R.Randall, *English Hunting in the Sixteenth Century*, Unpublished B.A. thesis, (University of Birmingham, 1980) pp.26-32.

33 R.Stewart-Brown, 'The Charter and Horn of the Master-Forester of Wirral', *T.H.S.L.C.*, Vol.87, (1935) p.107.

34 B.E.Harris (ed.) *V.C.H.*, Vol.II, (1979) pp.184-187. P.R.O., Palatinate of Chester Records, Plea Rolls, Chester 29/65 m2 (hereafter cited as *Ches. 29/65*). See P.H.W.Booth, 'Calendar of the Cheshire Trailbaston Proceedings, 1353', *Cheshire History*, No.11 (1983) p.47. (No.22).

35 Booth, *op. cit.*, p.48 (No.23).

36 Booth, *op. cit.*, p.49 (No.24).

37 Booth, *op. cit.*, p.49 (No.26).

38 See R.Stewart-Brown, 'The Charter and Horn of the Master-Forester of Wirral', *T.H.S.L.C.*, Vol.87, (1935).

39 See P.H.Booth, 'Taxation and Public Order : Cheshire in 1353', *Northern History* XII, (Leeds University, 1976) pp.16-31.

40 P.H.W.Booth, 'The End of Wirral Forest : An Anniversary, July 1376', *Cheshire History Newsletter*, No.12, (1977) pp.18-20.

41 H.M.S.O., *The Register of Edward the Black Prince*, Part III, (1932) p.458.

42 H.M.S.O., *The Register of Edward the Black Prince*, Part III, (1932) pp.401.

43 See E.H.Rideout, *The Growth of Wirral* (Liverpool, 1927) pp.95-6.

44 For institutions to vacant benefices in 1349, see H.J.Hewitt, *Mediaeval Cheshire*, Chet. Soc., 2nd Series, Vol.88, (1929) pp.178-9. For vacant tenancies, see P.H.W.Booth, *The Financial Administration of the Lordship and County of Chester, 1272-1377*, Chet. Soc., 3rd Series, Vol.28 (1981) p.3.

45 I.Kershaw, 'The Great Famine and Agrarian Crisis in England 1315-22', *Past and Present*, 59, (1973) pp.3-50.

46 The Subsidy Roll was transcribed by W.F.Irvine and published in *W.N. & Q.*, Vol.1, (1892) p.60 (No.109) et. seq.

47 D.Coleman, *The Economy of England 1450-1750* (Oxford, 1977) p.14

48 On lawlessness, see H.J.Hewitt, *Mediaeval Cheshire*, Chet. Soc., 2nd Series, Vol.88, (1929) pp.105-7.

49 *Ches. 29/65* No.85.

50 R.Stewart-Brown, *Birkenhead Priory and the Mersey Ferry* (Liverpool, 1925) pp.142-3.

51 See E.Rideout, 'The Sites of Ancient Villages in Wirral', *T.H.S.L.C.*, N.S., XLI, (1925) p.56.

52 J.Tait, (ed.) *The Chartulary, or Register of the Abbey of St. Werburgh*, Chet. Soc., N.S., Vol.82, Part 2 (1923) pp.377-8 (No.689).

53 There were exceptions to this, for example, Burton-in-Wirral.

54 See D.Sylvester, 'The Open Fields of Cheshire', *T.H.S.L.C.*, Vol.108 (1957) pp.1-33. 'Rural Settlement in Cheshire', *T.H.S.L.C.*, Vol.101 (1950) pp.1-12. P.H.W.Booth, 'Farming for Profit in the Fourteenth Century : The Cheshire Estates of the Earldom of Chester', *J.C.A.S.*, Vol.62, (1979) pp.75-6.

55 See G.Place, 'The Quest for a Market Charter', *Cheshire History*, Vol.5, (1980) pp.11-21.

56 In a study of the 1406 Communal Fine (Mize) and the 1545 Subsidy Roll, Ann Mabrey concluded that there was no evidence for the rise of Neston as the dominant community in Wirral. See 'Two Taxations in Wirral', *Cheshire History*, Vol.6, (1980) pp.28-45.

57 Wirral's present day population is 421,162. Source : County Monitor CEN 81 CM6 (1982). See also *V.C.H.*, Vol.II (1980) p.238.

58 For a list of Wirral water and windmills see E.Mitford Abraham, 'The Old Flour Mills of Wirral', *T.H.S.L.C.*, N.S., XIX, (1903) pp.133-149.

59 See R.J.de Little, *The Windmill, Yesterday and Today* (1972).

60 A.E.P.Gray, 'The Origin of Christianity in Wirral', *Journal of the British Archaeological Association*, Vol.XLIV, (1888) p.31. For early church history, see B.E.Harris (ed.) *V.C.H.*, Vol.III, (1980) pp.1-11.

61 J.Brownbill, 'Ancient Church Dedications in Cheshire and South Lancashire', *T.H.S.L.C.*, N.S., XVIII, (1902) pp.19-44.

62 See Charles Williams' article 'Wirral's Medieval Grave Slabs', in *The Wirral Journal*, Vol.1, No.6, (Upton, 1983) pp.34-6.

63 J.Tait (ed.) *The Chartulary, or Register of the Abbey of St. Werburgh, Chester*, Chet. Soc., 2nd Series, Vol.79, Part I (1920) pp.xvii-xviii.

64 R.W.Southern, *Western Church and Society in the Late Middle Ages* (Harmondsworth, 1970) pp.228-230.

65 By 1140 the Abbot held lands in Bebington, Greasby, Ness, Noctorum, West Kirby, Hilbre, Irby, Eastham (Bromborough), Upton, Barnston, Blacon, Great Caldy, Ledsham, Prenton, Storeton and Wallasey.

66 For example, a grant by Earl Ranulf III (1181-1232) relieved the Abbey of the payment of puture in all its Wirral lands, including its four demesne manors; Irby, Sutton, Eastham and Bromborough. Tait (ed.) *op. cit.*, pp.235-6 (No.353).

67 J.Tait (ed.) *The Chartulary, or Register of the Abbey of St. Werburgh* Chet. Soc., 2nd Series, Vol.82, Part 2, (1923) p.387 (No.696).

68 See C.Morris, *The Tudors* (1955) pp.81-6. For general background, see G.Elton, *England under the Tudors* (1955).

69 W.F.Irvine, *W.N. & Q.*, Vol.II, (1893) p.6 (No.166). M.E.C.Walcott, 'Inventories of Church Goods and Chantries in Cheshire Temp. Edward VI', *T.H.S.L.C.*, N.S., XI, (1870-1) pp.173-180.

70 A.G.Dickens, *The English Reformation* (2nd edition, 1967), p.174.

71 See below, pp.54.

72 For a history of the church in Cheshire, 1540-1660, see B.E.Harris (ed.) *V.C.H.*, Vol.III, (1980) pp.12-36. R.C.Richardson, *Puritanism in North-West England : A Regional Study of the Diocese of Chester to 1642* (Manchester, 1972).

73 See C.Haigh, *Reformation and Resistance in Tudor Lancashire* (Cambridge, 1975). J.Bossy, 'The Character of Elizabethan Catholicism', *Past and Present*, 21, (1962).

74 J.T.Driver, *Cheshire in the Later Middle Ages* (Chester, 1971) pp.128-131.

75 K.R.Wark, *Elizabethian Recusancy in Cheshire*, Chet. Soc., 3rd Series, Vol.19, (1971) p.10.

76 R.H.Morris, *Chester in the Plantagenet and Tudor Reigns* (Chester, 1894) pp.85-8.

77 *Ormerod*, pp.417-8.

78 J.Mayer, 'On the Arming of Levies in the Hundred of Wirral . . .', *T.H.S.L.C.*, XI, (1858-9) pp.83-96.

79 Wark *op. cit.*, pp.133.

80 *Calendar of State Papers, Domestic Series, of the Reigns of Elizabeth and James I, Addenda, 1580-1625* (ed. M.A.E.Green), Vol.XXVI, (1872) p.35 (No.94).

81 See F.Sanders, 'Bishop Chadderton's Visitation Articles 1581', *J.C.A.S.*, N.S., XIII, (1907) pp.5-25.

82 K.Thomas, *Religion and the Decline of Magic* (1971).

83 J.Beck, *Tudor Cheshire* (Chester, 1969) p.84.

84 *W.N. & Q.*, Vol.II, (1893) pp.248-9 (No. 241), *op. cit.*, p.52 (No.247).

85 *W.N. & Q.*, Vol.II, (1893) p.53 (No. 247).

86 *W.N. & Q.*, Vol.II, (1893) pp.64-5 (No.265).

87 *V.C.H.* Vol.III, (1890) p.32.

88 Quoted in G.P.Higgins, 'The Government of Early Stuart Cheshire 1590-1640', *Northern History*, XII, (Leeds University, 1976) p.42. cf. K.P.Wark's comments that the existing evidence suggests little religious conservatism or recusancy in Cheshire. (*op. cit.*, pp.10-11). The bishop's visitation books for 1554 list all clergy and churchwardens throughout the diocese; the continuity is noticeable. Thomas Sharpe, rector of Thurstaston, was presented to the living in Henry VIII's time and continued until his resignation in 1601. (See *W.N. & Q.*, Vol.II, (1893) p.59 (No.258).

89 See *W.N. & Q.*, Vol.I, (1892) p.80 (No.141), for list of Wirral gentry in 1579. (See also revised list in *W.N. & Q.*, Vol.II, (1893) pp.85-6 (No.288).

90 See below, pp.122.

91 W.F.Irvine, 'The Early Stanleys', *T.H.S.L.C.*, Vol.105 (1954) pp.45-68.

92 J.Brownbill, 'The Troutbeck Family', *J.C.A.S.*, N.S., Vol.28, Part 2, (1929) pp.149-79.

93 See *W.N. & Q.*, Vol.I, (1892) p.65 (No.118). For list of Whitmore recusants, see Wark, *op. cit.*, pp.168-170.

94 *Mortimer*, p.169.

95 For example, see the pioneering works of W.G.Hoskins, *Local History in England* (2nd Edition, 1972) pp.119-138, *Fieldwork in Local History* (2nd Edition, 1982) pp.23-4, 94-106. For local building types, see W.A.Singleton, 'Traditional House-Types in

Rural Lancashire and Cheshire', *T.H.S.L.C.*, Vol.104, (1952) pp.75-91. L.McKenna, 'An Outline of the Development of the Timber Frame in Cheshire', *Cheshire History*, No.10 (1982) pp.39-52.

96 See A.A.Shatwell, *The Cruck-Built Barn of Vineyard Farm, Poulton-Lancelyn, Wirral,* Unpublished B.A. thesis (University of Liverpool, 1977).

97 D.J.Hoey, 'Three Cruck Buildings in Lancashire and Cheshire', *T.H.S.L.C.*, Vol.117 (1965) pp.53-7.

98 See J.H.Harvey, *'Sources for the History of Houses',* British Records Association, Archives and the User, No.3, (1974). F.C.Beazley, 'Inscribed House Plates in the Hundred of Wirral', *Cheshire Sheaf,* 3rd Series, Vol.VII, (1909) No.1192 et. seq.

99 See N.Davey, *A History of Building Materials,* (1961) A Clifton-Taylor, *The Pattern of English Building,* (2nd Edition, 1972).

100 W.G.Hoskins, 'The Rebuilding of Rural England 1570-1649', *Past & Present*, No.4, (1953).

101 R.Foster, *Discovering English Churches* (1981) p.7.

102 F.H.Crossley, 'Cheshire Church Towers', *J.C.A.S.*, N.S., XXXI, (1936) p.90. See also, 'Cheshire Churches in the Twelfth Century', *J.C.A.S.* N.S., XXXII, Part II, (1938) pp.73-97.

103 See F.H.Crossley, 'The Renaissance of Cheshire Church Building in the Late Fifteenth and Early Sixteenth Centuries', *J.C.A.S.* N.S., XXXIV, Part II, (1940) pp.53-160. 'On The Importance of Fourteenth Century Planning in the Construction of the Churches of Cheshire', *J.C.A.S.* N.S., XXXII, Part I, (1937) pp.5-52.

104 R.Richards, *Old Cheshire Churches* (2nd Edition, 1973) p.47.

105 *V.C.H.*, Vol.III, (1980) pp.12-36.

106 W.G.Hoskins, *Local History in England* (2nd Edition, 1972) p.60. J.W.Ellis, 'The Mediaeval Fonts of the Hundreds of West Derby and Wirral', *T.H.S.L.C.*,N.S., XVII, (1901) pp.73-80.

107 For bell inscriptions, see *W.N. & Q.*, Vol.II, (1893) p.7 (No.169) et. seq.

Chapter II: Wallasey and North Wirral

1 An alternative explanation for the place-name is put forward by Susan Craggs. She thinks that the Norman *Walea* may signify 'cliff island' reflecting the general lie of the land. For early Christianity, see W.F.Irvine, 'Notes on Parish Churches', *T.H.S.L.C.*,N.S., XI, (1895) p.114.

2 The course was in existence from at least the early seventeenth century. In King's *Vale Royal* (c.1615-16) Wallasey is described as a town with 'fair lands . . . which for the fitness of such a purpose, allure the gentlemen and others oft to appoint great matches, and venture no small sums, in trying the swiftness of their horses.' (reproduced as an Appendix to *Mortimer*, pp.10-15). See also, *W.N. & Q.*, Vol.II (1893), pp.86-87 (No.289).

3 H.Gamlin, *'Twixt Mersey and Dee* (Liverpool, 1897) p.124.

4 W.F.Irvine, 'Notes on the Old Halls of Wirral', *T.H.S.L.C.*, N.S., XVII, (1901) p.97.

5 For smuggling and Mother Redcap's, see E.C.Woods & P.C.Brown, *The Rise and Progress of Wallasey* (3rd Edition, Wallasey, 1974) hereafter cited as *R & P*, pp.113-120 ; pp.121-128. E.C.Woods, 'Smuggling in Wirral', *T.H.S.L.C.*, Vol.79, (1927) pp.119-135.

6 *Wallasey News,* 8 December 1973. See also Alan Brack's comments in *The Wirral* (1980) p.47.

7 W.F.Irvine, 'Notes on the Old Halls of Wirral', *T.H.S.L.C.*, N.S., XVII, (1901) pp.94-7.

8 For description of Leasowe Castle see *R & P*, pp.99-112. E.C.Woods, 'Leasowe Castle ; Its Owners and History', *T.H.S.L.C.*, N.S., XXXVII, (1921) pp.127-148 'Why was Leasowe Castle built?', *Cheshire Sheaf*, 3rd Series, Vol.6, (1906) No.1096. T.Ling, *The Castle by the Sea* (1912).

9 See R.D.Radcliffe, *An Old Racing Stable at Wallasey in Wirral* (Liverpool, 1894). Also in *T.H.S.L.C.*, N.S., IX, (1893) pp.141-158. According to Mrs.Gamlin (1897) the stables resembled the architecture of Bidston Hall, a small manor house of early seventeenth-century origin.

10 Advertisement in *London Gazette,* February 12-15, 1671. The Duke of Monmouth, illegitimate son of Charles II, visited Leasowe, in 1682 — ostensibly for racing, but really to gather support. See J.P.Earwaker, 'The 'Progress' of the Duke of Monmouth in Cheshire, in September 1682', *T.H.S.L.C.*, N.S., X, (1894) pp.71-96. Gamlin, *op. cit.*, pp.120-125.

11 *R & P*, p.102.

12 *The Contents of Leasowe Castle, Leasowe, Cheshire,* Catalogue of Sale, September 16-17 1893.

13 Mr.R.Shaw, Director of Development, Wirral Borough Council, quoted in *Liverpool Daily Post,* 2 August 1979.

14 In a survey of Bidston, dated 1665, a circular churchyard is shown. Circular or oval enclosures appear to be characteristic of early church foundations. See G.Chitty, 'Wirral Rural Fringes Survey Report', *J.M.A.S.*, Vol. 2 (1978) p.8.

15 According to Robinson in his *Account of Wallasey* (c.1727) reproduced as Appendix II to *R & P*, pp.351-360. See also W.C.Ashby Pritt, 'An Account of Wallasey, based on that of Mr Henry Robinson, school-master there, 1720; with Notes on the Parish and Extracts from the Registers', *T.H.S.L.C.*, N.S., VII & VIII, (1891-2) pp.1-62.

16 For a full account of the nineteenth-century finds, together with a conjectural plan of the mediaeval church, see E.W.Cox, 'Notes on the History of Wallasey Church'; *J.C.A.S.*, N.S., Vol.1, (1887) pp.53-75. For the Norman font, see J.W.Ellis, 'The Mediaeval Fonts of the Hundreds of West Derby and Wirral', *T.H.S.L.C.*, N.S.,XVII, (1901) pp.73-4.

17 J.Brownbill, *West Kirby and Hilbre* (Liverpool, 1927) p.267.

18 *Liverpool Post,* February 2, 1857.

19 The parish registers have been partly transcribed by E.M.Hance & T.N.Morton, 'Extracts from the Parish Registers of the Parish Church of St. Hilary, Wallasey, with Notes thereupon', *T.H.S.L.C.*, XXXV, (1882-3) pp.37-111.

20 Robinson, *op. cit.*

21 F.R.Raines (ed.) *Notitia Cestriensis, Chet. Soc.,* 1st Series, VIII (1845) pp.175-6.

22 See *R & P*, pp.66-7 for the possible existence of a mediaeval manor.

23 A.Hume, 'Changes in the Sea Coast of Lancashire and Cheshire', *T.H.S.L.C.*, N.S., VI, (1865-6) pp.36-7. The Williamson Art Gallery & Museum, Birkenhead, has a mediaeval grave slab discovered during the construction of the Leasowe/Meols embankment.

24 J.Tait (ed.) *The Chartulary or Register of the Abbey of St. Werburgh, Chester, Chet. Soc.,* N.S., Vol.79 Part I (1920) pp.127-8 (No.96).

25 See below, p.140.

26 They were incorporated in the County Borough of Wallasey in 1928. Until 1863 they were part of Bidston parish.

27 A.Mabrey, 'Two Taxations in Wirral', *Cheshire History,* Vol.6 (1980) pp.28-45.

28 W.F.Irvine in 'Notes on the Ancient Parish of Bidston', *T.H.S.L.C.*, N.S., IX, (1893) p.178, noted the existence in Moreton of 'Priory Field' and 'Dovehouse Yard'.

29 See J.Brownbill, 'A History of the Old Parish of Bidston, Cheshire', *T.H.S.L.C.*, Vol.88, (1936) pp.71-102; 103-104.

30 A.Hume, 'Outline of the Sea Coast of Cheshire', *T.H.S.L.C.*, XI, (1858-9) pp.219-232. C.Potter, 'Observations of the Geology and Archaeology of Cheshire Shore', *T.H.S.L.C.*, 3rd Series, IV, (1875-6) pp.121-142. E.W.Cox, 'Traces of Submerged Lands on the Coasts of Lancashire, Cheshire and North Wales', *T.H.S.L.C.*, N.S., X, (1894) pp.19-56. R.Kenna, 'Early Settlement in the North Wirral Coastal Area', *J.M.A.S.*, Vol.2 (1978) pp.27-34. G.Chitty, 'Wirral Rural Fringes Survey Report', *J.M.A.S.*, Vol.2, (1978) pp. 4-6., 14. R. Kenna, 'An old woodland floor beneath the sea', *The Wirral Journal*, Vol.2, No.8 (Upton, 1985) pp. 26-30.

31 For a summary of the finds, with bibliography, see G.Chitty and M.Warhurst, 'Ancient Meols ; A Collection of Finds from the Cheshire Shore in Merseyside County Museums', *J.M.A.S.*, Vol.I, (1977) pp.19-42. Many of the nineteenth-century finds were catalogued and illustrated in A.Hume, *Ancient Meols* (1863). See also, H.E.Smith, 'Archaeology of the Mersey District 1866', *T.H.S.L.C.*, N.S., VII, (1866-7) pp.178-188 et.seq. C.Potter, 'Antiquities of the Meols Shore', *T.H.S.L.C.*, N.S., IV, (1888) pp.143-152. 'Leather, Bronze, Pewter, & c. Ornaments from the Cheshire Shore', *T.H.S.L.C.*, N.S., V, (1889) pp.195-202. 'Agricultural and Mechanical Implements found on the Meols Shore', *T.H.S.L.C.*, N.S., VII & VIII, (1891-2) pp.233-244. F.W.Longbottom, 'A Few Notes on the Coins of the Potter Meols Collection', *J.C.A.S.*, N.S., XIV, (1908) pp.5-17.

32 A.Hume, *Ancient Meols* (1863) p.26.

33 Hume, *op. cit.,* p.286.

34 G.Chitty and M.Warhurst, 'Ancient Meols', *J.M.A.S.*, Vol.I, (1977) p.21. See J.D.Bu'Lock, 'The Celtic, Saxon and Scandinavian Settlement at Meols in Wirral', *T.H.S.L.C.*, Vol.112, (1960) pp.1-28.

35 G.Lloyd-Morgan, *Roman Finds from Meols*, unpublished MS, (1980). I am grateful to Dr. Lloyd-Morgan for her help with my section on Meols, and for the supply of her unpublished material on coins and bells.

36 R.H.M.Dolley, 'The Anglo-Saxon Coins from Meols Sands', *T.H.S.L.C.*, Vol.113, (1961) pp.197-201.

37 F.H.Thompson, *Roman Cheshire* (Chester, 1965) p.98.

38 Early maps show a considerable projection seawards at Meols, for example that of Captain Grenville Collins published in 1689. In the nineteenth-century, skeletons were found off the coast, near Leasowe Lighthouse, and a grave slab and skeleton of 'prehistoric man' was discovered near Leasowe Castle.

39 E.W.Cox, 'Ancient Houses on Meols Shore', *T.H.S.L.C.*, N.S., XI, (1895) p.248.

Chapter III: Birkenhead, Bebington and Bromborough

1 P.Sulley, *History of Ancient and Modern Birkenhead* (Liverpool, 1907) p.48.

2 J.Brownbill, 'A History of the Old Parish of Bidston, Cheshire', *T.H.S.L.C.*, Vol.87, (1935) p.159.

3 Birkenhead proper is some three miles from the mouth, and eight from the head or source of the Birket.

4 See C.Aldridge, 'The Priory of the Blessed Virgin and Saint James, Birkenhead', *T.H.S.L.C.*, N.S., VI, (1890) p.145.

5 See *Ormerod*, p.462. R.Stewart-Brown,, *Birkenhead Priory and the Mersey Ferry* (Liverpool, 1925) pp.24-6.

6 Stewart-Brown, *op. cit.,* pp.54-5.

7   The original village of Claughton was probably situated at the junction of Park Road South and Palm Hill. The field-name, Moat Croft, near Park Station, suggests the possibility of another grange. (See W.F.Irvine, 'Notes on the Ancient Parish of Bidston', *T.H.S.L.C.*, N.S., IX, (1893) p.78.

8   T.Heywood, (ed.), *The Moore Rental,* Chet. Soc.,, 1st Series, XII, (1857) p.36.

9   *V.C.H.,* Vol.III, (1980) p.130.

10   *V.C.H.,* Vol.III (1980) p.130.

11   Stewart-Brown, *op. cit.,* p.92. The commissioners' report is reproduced in *Mortimer,* p.317-8.

12   *Letters and Papers Foreign and Domestic Henry VIII* (ed. J.Gairdner), Vol.VIII, Part I, (1892) p.576.

13   The traditional inference is that they took to book-binding, based upon a rather vague entry in the Liverpool Town Books.

14   See A.G.Dickens, *The English Reformation* (2nd Edition, 1967) pp.197-232.

15   A rental of 1536 lists the priory's holdings prior to the grant to Worsely. (See *W.N. & Q.,* Vol.2, (1893) p.39. (No.221) et. seq. For the grant to Worsley, see W.F.Irvine,, *Cheshire Sheaf,* 3rd Series, Vol.XX, (1923) pp.6-8 (No.4708). Also, *Letters and Papers Foreign and Domestic Henry VIII* (ed. J.Gairdner & R.H.Brodie), Vol.XX, Part I, (1905) p.217 (No.49).

16   *Mortimer,* p.321.

17   For the nineteenth-century restoration, see A.M.Robinson, 'The Birkenhead Priory Reparation', *T.H.S.L.C.*, N.S., XIX & XX, (1903-4) pp.107-113. See also, E.W.Cox, 'Birkenhead Priory', *T.H.S.L.C.*, N.S., X, (1894) pp.123-156.

18   The similarity to Chester Cathedral extends to the chapter house and monks' dormitory.

19   The inscription (in Latin) reads, 'Here lieth Thomas Raynford a former worthy prior of this house who died on the eighth of May in the year of our Lord 1473.' Three skeletons were found beneath this stone, 'the teeth in particular were in a high state of preservation.' (*Mortimer,* p.315).

20   Ormerod thought the former, Harold Brakspear (in Stewart-Brown, *op. cit.,* pp.106-126) the latter.

21   See Stewart-Brown, *op. cit.,* pp.18-21.

22   Aldridge, *op. cit.,* pp.141-160.

23   See W.F.Bushell, 'The Ancient Graveyard of Birkenhead Priory', *T.H.S.L.C.*, Vol.108, (1956) pp.141-6.

24   *Mortimer,* p.309.

25   *Mortimer,* p.310.

26   *Stewart-Brown, op. cit.,* p.133.

27   See *Cheshire Sheaf,* 1st Series, Vol.II (1881) p.253-4.

28   Stewart-Brown, *op. cit.,* p.163.

29   Stewart-Brown, *op. cit.,* p.171.

30   See W.F.Irvine, *W.N. & Q.,* Vol.2, (1893) pp.8-9 (No.171).

31   Irvine, *op. cit.;* the earliest known reference to an enclosing wall at Bidston appears in a lease of 1609. The wall was traditionally known as 'Penny-a-day Dyke' — possibly a reference to the wages of those who built it. For the importance of the deer park in litigation over Bidston, see E.B.Goodawe, 'Three Notes on Bidston and the Stanleys', *T.H.S.L.C.*, Vol.91, (1939) pp.166.174.

32   See *The Egerton Papers,* Camden Society, (1860) pp.96-7.

33   See above, p.44.

34   See H.Hughes, *Cheshire and its Welsh Borders,* (1966) pp.91-4.

35   See F.H.Cheetham in J.Brownbill, 'A History of the Old Parish of Bidston, Cheshire', *T.H.S.L.C.*, Vol.88, (1936) pp.61-70.

36   A.Smith, *Christopher Tadpole* (1847-8).

37   See E.C.Woods & P.C.Brown, *The Rise and Progress of Wallasey* (3rd Edition, Wallasey, 1974) pp.126-8.

38   E.W.Cox in *W.N. & Q.,* Vol.1, (1892) p.14 (No.23).

39   Ormerod, p.468. J.C.Atkinson (ed.) *Notes on the Churches of Cheshire by the Late Sir Stephen Glynne,* Chet. Soc., 2nd Series, XXXII, (1884) p.60. See also F.H.Cheetham in J.Brownbill, 'A History of the Old Parish of Bidston, Cheshire', *T.H.S.L.C.*, Vol.88, (1936) pp.19-45.

40   The tower has been compared to that at Wallasey, which is dated 1530.

41   This interpretation is based upon W.F.Irvine, 'Notes on the Ancient Parish of Bidston, *T.H.S.L.C.*, N.S., IX, (1893) p.53.

42   W.F.Irvine, *The Baptismal, Marriage, and Burial Registers of the Parish of Bidston, Cheshire, 1581-1700* (Liverpool, 1893) Also in *W.N. & Q.,* Vol.1, (1892) p.2 (No.2) et. seq.

43   W.F.Irvine, 'Notes on the Parish Churches of Wirral', *T.H.S.L.C.*, N.S., XL, (1924) p.121.

44   See H.B.Neilson, *Auld Lang Syne : Recollections and Rural Records of Old Claughton, Birkenhead and Bidston with Other Reminiscences* (Birkenhead, 1935) pp.186-8.

45   *The Vale Royal of England or the County Palatine of Chester* (published by Daniel King in 1656) reproduced in *Mortimer* (Appendix p.13).

46   Several Elizabethan writers noted the trend. For example, in 1592 Francis Bacon wrote that 'There was never the like number of fine and stately houses as have been built and set up from the ground since her Majesty's reign.' See W.G.Hoskins' seminal essay, 'The Rebuilding of Rural England, 1570-1640', *Past & Present,* No.4, (1953) reprinted in *Provincial England* (1961).

47   See E.H.Goodawe, *op. cit.,* pp.165-6. W.F.Irvine, 'Notes on the 'Ancient Parish of Bidston', *T.H.S.L.C.*, N.S., IX (1893) pp.33-7.

48   Near to this site, south-east of Bidston Hall, there is a circular hollow said to be the old cockpit. The Stanley family were well known in the seventeenth-century for their fighting fowl.

49   A drawing of the hall appears in the Kingston survey of Bidston, dated 1665 (and now in the possession of the Vyner family). Max Faulkner's restoration programme in 1966 envisaged the reinstatement of the hall's original roof lines; this was abandoned due to heavy costs. Instead, the two wider slated roofs running north and south were restored. (See, M.Faulkner, *An Appeal for Survival* (Birkenhead, 1971) p.18). For a detailed description of Bidston Hall, see F.H.Cheetham in J.Brownbill, 'A History of the Old Parish of Bidston, Cheshire', *T.H.S.L.C.,* Vol.88, (1936) pp.61-70.

50   For Bidston as a Conservation Area, see below, p.132.

51   The deed, discovered in 1950, is printed in B.H.C.Turvey, *Notes on the History of Woodchurch* (Birkenhead, 1954) p.47. For a history of Woodchurch, see W.F.Irvine and F.C.Beazley, 'Notes on the Parish of Woodchurch', *T.H.S.L.C.,* N.S., XVII, (1901) pp.139-178.

52   F.H.Crossley, 'Church Building in Cheshire during the Thirteenth Century', *T.H.S.L.C.,* Vol.95, (1943) p.37.

53   See W.W.Mortimer, 'Memoir of the Family of Holme, especially of the various Randle Holmes; the Cheshire Antiquaries of the Seventeenth Century', *T.H.S.L.C.,* 1st Series, I, (1849) pp.86-94.

54   J.E.Allison, *Sidelights on Tranmere* (Birkenhead, 1976) pp.18-19.

55   P.Sulley, *History of Ancient and Modern Birkenhead* (Liverpool, 1907) p.341.

56   Allison, *op. cit.,* pp.22-3.

57   J.Mayer, 'On the Old Halls of Cheshire No.1 Tranmere Hall', *T.H.S.L.C.,* 1st Series, III, (1850-1) p.108.

58   For a full account, see Allison, *op. cit.,* pp.25-7.

59   G.E.Connah, *The Old Houses of Bebington* (Essay Prize for Local History, Bebington Rotary Club 1952) p.3.

60   E.W.Cox, 'Leaves from an Antiquary's Note Book', *T.H.S.L.C.,* N.S., XII, (1896) p.255.

61   R.Richards, *Old Cheshire Churches* (2nd Edition, 1973) p.47.

62   N.Hawthorne, *English Note-Books* (1853-60) ed. G.P.Lathrop, *Our Old House and English Note-Books* (Standard Library edition, Vol.VII, 1891).

63   See E.W.Cox, 'A Pre-Norman Church at Bebington', *Cheshire Sheaf,* 3rd Series, Vol.1 (1896) pp.45-7. (No.49).

64   E.W.Cox, 'The Architectural History of Bebington Church', *T.H.S.L.C.,* N.S., XIII, (1897) pp.97-121.

65   Cox, 'The Architectural History of Bebington Church', *T.H.S.L.C.,* N.S., XII, (1897) p.105.

66   R.Richards, *Old Cheshire Churches* (2nd Edition, 1973) p.48.

67   See H.E.Smith, 'Archaeology in the Mersey District 1867', *T.H.S.L.C.,* N.S., VIII, (1867-8) pp.98-9.

68   J.Tait (ed.) *The Chartulary or Register of the Abbey of St. Werburgh, Chester,* Chet. Soc., N.S., Vol.79, Part 1, (1920) p.248 (No.387).

69   Tait *op. cit.,* Vol.82, Part 2, (1923) pp.375-7. (No.668).

70   Tait, *op. cit.,* Vol. 82, Part 2, (1923) pp.297-8. (No.517 et. seq.).

71   Tait, *op. cit.,* Vol. 79, Part 1, (1920) p.126. (No.91).

72   The existence of a monastery is mentioned by *Mortimer* (p.207) amongst others, and this supposition is based upon entries in the Anglo-Saxon Chronicle.

73   See T.T.Wilkinson, 'On the Battle of Brunanburgh, and the Probable Locality of the Conflict', *T.H.S.L.C.,* 1st Series, Vol.IX, (1856-7) pp.21-41. J.McN.Dodgson, 'The Background of Brunanburh', *Saga Book of the Viking Society for Northern Research,* Vol.IV, Part IV, (1956-7) pp.303-16.

74   *Sulley,* p.208. See *The Bromborough Society 19th Annual Report* (1951-2).

75   Tait, *op. cit.,* Vol.79, Part 1, (1920) p.114 (No.68).

76   Tait, *op. cit.,* Vol.79, Part 1, (1920) pp.212-3. (No.318).

77   G.Chitty et. al., 'Report 2 Bromborough Court House A Survey of the Evidence', *Merseyside Archaeological Society* (Liverpool, 1979) pp.6-8, 15.

78   D.Freke, 'Bromborough Court House Moated Site Excavations 1979', *J.M.A.S.,* Vol.2, (1978) pp.47-52.

79   G.E.Connah, *The Old Houses of Bebington* (Essay Prize for Local History, Bebington Rotary Club 1952) p.10.

80   For a brief summary of Bromborough's manor houses, see K.Jones, 'Bromborough Manor Houses', *J.M.A.S.,* Vol.2, (1978) pp.35-6.

81   W.Hewitt, *The Wirral Peninsula* (Liverpool, 1922) p.183.

82   For a full account of these carvings see A.Anderson, 'The Manor House Farm', in *The Bromborough Society 22nd Annual Report,* (1954-5).

83   See *Cheshire Sheaf,* 3rd Series, XXIX, (1944) pp.83-5 (No.8450) et. seq.

Chapter IV: Villages of Wirral

1 *Greasby Report,* (Liverpool University, 1965) p.5.

2 J.Tait, *The Chartulary or Register of the Abbey of St. Werburgh, Chester', Chet. Soc.,* N.S., Vol.79, Part 1, (1920) pp.78-9 (No.23). For the manor's descent, see J.Brownbill, *West Kirby and Hilbre* (Liverpool, 1928) pp.281-296. For an outline of Greasby's history, J.Williams, *The Story of Greasby* (Greasby, 1978).

3 See J.T.O'Neil, *Operation Pump Lane* (Hoylake, 1982).

4 O'Neil, *op. cit.,* pp.1-2. P.France, *A Roman Road in Wirral,* Unpublished notes, (1964).

5 W.T.Watkin, *Roman Cheshire* (Liverpool, 1886; reprint with introduction by D.F.Petch, Wakefield, 1974) p.59.

6 See Brownbill, *op. cit.,* pp.218-234.

7 G.Chitty, 'Wirral Rural Fringes Survey Report', *J.M.A.S.,* Vol.2, N.S.,(1978) p.12.

8 N.Ellison, *The Wirral Peninsula* (1955) p.79.

9 See G.Chitty, 'Irby Mill Excavations 1979', *J.M.A.S.,* Vol.2, (1978) pp.37-45.

10 See E.M.Abraham , 'The Old Flour Mills of Wirral', *T.H.S.L.C.,* N.S., XIX, (1903) pp.133-149.

11 E.W.Cox, 'The Antiquities of Storeton in Wirral', *T.H.S.L.C.,* N.S., XIII, (1897) p.50.

12 W.F.Irvine, 'Notes on the Old Halls of Wirral', *T.H.S.L.C.,* N.S., XVII, (1901) p.102.

13 R.Stewart-Brown, 'The Charter and Horn of the Master-Forester of Wirral', *T.H.S.L.C.,* Vol.87, (1935) pp.97-112.

14 His second eldest son, Sir John Stanley, Lord Deputy of Ireland, married Isabella, the heiress of Lathom, and founder of the families of the Earl of Derby and Lord Stanley of Alderley.

15 Cox, *op. cit.,* p.68.

16 Cox, *op. cit.,* p.65.

17 See E.E.Barber, *Talbot Deeds 1200-1682, Rec. Soc.,* Vol.103, (1948) pp.1-10.

18 See J.Brownbill, 'The Troutbeck Family' *J.C.A.S.,* N.S., Vol.28, Part 2, (1929) pp.149-179.

19 Barber, *op. cit.,* p.2.

20 P.H.W.Booth, 'Calendar of the Cheshire Trailbaston Proceedings, 1353', *Cheshire History,* No.11, (1983) p.45. (No.20).

21 Booth, *op. cit.*

22 Edward Hubbard in N.Pevsner and E.Hubbard, *Cheshire* (The Buildings of England Series, Harmondsworth, 1971) p.115.

23 *Mortimer,* p.212.

24 E.W.Cox, 'Leaves from an Antiquary's Note-Book', *T.H.S.L.C.,* N.S., XI, (1895) pp.250-2.

25 See Tait, *op. cit.,* Vol.79, Part 1, (1920) pp.233-5. (No.351).

26 Ellison, *op. cit.,* p.227.

27 W.F.Irvine, 'Place-Names in the Hundred of Wirral', *T.H.S.L.C.,* N.S., II & III, (1891-2) pp.279-304.

28 K.E.Jermy, 'The Roman Road in Wirral', *J.C.A.S.,* Vol.48, (1961) pp.1-13.

29 E.H.Rideout, 'Wirral Field Names', *T.H.S.L.C.,* Vol.XL, (1924) pp.130-1.

30 W.Hewitt, *The Wirral Peninsula* (Liverpool, 1922) p.182.

31 See D.Morris, 'Willaston — New Light on an Old Wirral Village' *Cheshire History,* Vol.5, (1980) pp.22-33.

32 See below, pp.133-134.

33 *Sulley* p.194.

34 N.Hawthorne, *English Note-Books* (1953-60) ed. G.P.Lathrop, *Our Old House and English Note-Books* (Standard Library edition, Vol.VII, 1891) pp.493-4.

35 See below, pp.135, 140.

36 See below, p.135.

37 E.C.Bryan, *Willaston's Heritage* (Willaston, 1975) p.26.

Chapter V: The Dee Estuary

1 K.P.Wilson, *The Port of Chester in the Late Middle Ages,* (University of Liverpool PhD Thesis, 2 Vols., 1965). K.P.Wilson (ed.) *Chester Customs Accounts 1301-1566, Rec. Soc.,* Vol.CXI, (1969). R.H.Morris, *Chester in the Plantaganet and Tudor Reigns* (Chester, 1894) pp.457-479. For a list of Wirral vessels trading at Chester in the sixteenth-century, see *W.N. & Q.,* Vol.1, (1892) p.16 (No.26) et. seq.

2 Cf. K.P.Wilson, 'The Port of Chester in the Fifteenth Century', *T.H.S.L.C.,* Vol.117, (1965) pp.1-15.

3 Quoted in J.Beck, *Tudor Cheshire* (Chester, 1969) p.8.

4 K.P.Wilson (ed.) *Chester Customs Accounts 1301-1566, Rec. Soc.,* Vol.CXI, (1969) p.4.

5 Wilson, *op. cit.,* pp.8-16.

6 Beck, *op. cit.,* p.7.

7 Morris, *op. cit.,* pp.459-462.

8 F.Simpson, 'The River Dee', *J.C.A.S.,* N.S., XIV, (1908) pp.85-111.

9 J.Brownbill, *West Kirby and Hilbre* (Liverpool, 1928) p.158.

10 J.Tait, (ed.) *The Chartulary or Register of the Abbey of St. Werburgh, Chester, Chet. Soc.,* Vol.82, Part 2, (1923) pp.289-290 (No.504) et. seq.

11 Tait, *op. cit.,* pp.293-4 (No.510) et. seq.

12 See Collingwood in Brownbill, *op. cit.,* pp.14-26.

13 See H.E.Smith, 'Archaeology in the Mersey District 1869', *T.H.S.L.C.,* N.S., X, (1869-70) pp.270-2. 'Reliques of the Anglo-Saxon Churches of St. Bridget and St. Hildeburga, West Kirby, Cheshire', *T.H.S.L.C.,* N.S., XI, (1870-1) pp.13-46.

14 See T.Moore, 'Some Notes on the Parish of West Kirkby, in the Hundred of Wirrall, *T.H.S.L.C.,* 1st Series, Vol.VII, (1854-5) pp.12-16. F.H.Cheetham in Brownbill, *op. cit.,* pp.125-150.

15 R.Richards, *Old Cheshire Churches* (2nd Edition, 1973) p.349.

16 The heraldry has not been satisfactorily explained. W.F.Irvine in 'Notes on the Parish Churches of Wirral', *T.H.S.L.C.,* N.S., XI, (1895) pp.135-6, suggested that the shields may represent the Meols family, Banastre of Bank, Bishop Smith, (Bishop of Lichfield and Coventry 1493-5) and the Debenham or Debnam family. This last is puzzling, as there is no record of such a family in West Kirby. See also J.P.Rylands in C.D.Brown, 'The Ancient Parish of West Kirby', *T.H.S.L.C.,* N.S., I, (1885) pp.66-7.

17 E.W.Cox, *W.N. & Q.,* Vol.2, (1893) p.3 (No.160).

18 See *Mortimer,* pp.163-4.

19 *Sulley,* p.248.

20 See H.E.Smith, 'Notice of an Early Conventual Cemetery in Wirral, *T.H.S.L.C.,* N.S., V, (1864-5) pp.271-6. A.Hume, 'The Hilbre Cross', *T.H.S.L.C.,* N.S., III, (1862-3) pp.233-4.

21 R.Newstead, 'The Excavations at Hilbre 1926', *T.H.S.L.C.,* N.S., XLII, (1926) pp.136-143.

22 Newstead, *op. cit.,* p.141.

23 See the Department of Leisure Services' leaflet 'Discovering Wirral's Countryside: Hilbre'.

24 Wirral Borough Council, 'Report on the Islands of Hilbre', October 1976, p.8.

25 F.C.Beazley, *Thurstaston in Cheshire : An Account of the Parish, Manor and Church,* (Liverpool, 1924), reprinted from *T.H.S.L.C.,* N.S., XXXIX, (1923) pp.1-177.

26 See J.Picton in *Cheshire Sheaf,* 1st Series, Vol.8, (1877) p.364 and *ibid.,* Vol.3, (1881) p.30.

27 Quoted in W.F.Irvine, 'The Early Stanleys', *T.H.S.L.C.,* Vol.105, (1953) pp.45-68.

28 *Sulley,* p.86. *Mortimer,* p.264.

29 Sites and Monuments Record, Merseyside County Museums, Ref. 2484;5 (18.9.80).

30 *Cheshire Sheaf,* Third Series, LIV, (1959) p.13.

31 D.Lysons and S.Lysons, *Magna Britannia,* Vol.2, (1810) p.804.

32 See *W.N. & Q.,* Vol.2, (1893) p.68. (No.270) et. seq.

33 See K.Lee, *St.Peter's Church and Parish, Heswall: A Short History and Guide* (Heswall, 1979).

34 See F.H.Crossley, 'The Post-Reformation Effigies and Monuments of Cheshire', *T.H.S.L.C.,* Vol.91, (1939) p.72. For parish registers, see T.H.May, *The Registers of Baptisms, Marriages and Burials in the Parish of Heswall 1559-1729,* (Guildford, 1896).

35 *Ormerod,* p.513.

36 The London Gazette reported in 1690 that William III slept at the Hall, on his way to Ireland.

37 *Ormerod,* p.535.

38 *Ormerod,* p.535.

39 See H.E.Smith, 'Archaeology of the Mersey District 1874', *T.H.S.L.C.,* Third Series, III, (1874-5) pp.85-95. See above, pp.23.

Chapter VI: Eastham and South Wirral

1 N.Hawthorne, *English Note-Books* (1853-60) ed. G.P.Lathrop, *Our Old House and English Note-Books* (Standard Library edition, Vol.VII, 1891) p.491.

2 M.E.London, 'Landing Places used by the Eastham Ferry Boats', *Cheshire History Newsletter,* No.12, (1977) pp.21-3., No.13, (1977) pp.6-9.

3 See J.P.Rylands, 'Armorial Panels in Eastham Church', *T.H.S.L.C.,* N.S., XXV, (1909) pp.212-3. W.F.J.Timbrell, 'The Mediaeval Stall-End in Hawarden Church and Contemporary Panels in Eastham Church', *J.C.A.S.,* N.S., XXIII, (1920) pp.37-42.

4 H.J.Storrs in I.Tobin, *The Parish of Eastham* (Liverpool, 1920) p.52.

5 Correspondence between Alan Mitchell of the Forestry Commission and Alan Brack.

6 N.Ellison, *The Wirral Peninsula* (1955) p.158.

7 *Mortimer,* p.227.

8 On the evidence of a chimney-piece in the Great Hall. See the description in *Ormerod,* pp.422-3; also, M.E.Poole, 'The Poole Family of Poole Hall in Wirral', *T.H.S.L.C.,* N.S., XVI, (1900) pp.172-4.

9 Poole, *op. cit.,* pp.165-216.

10 *Ormerod,* p.425.

11 R.N.Jones and P.H.W.Booth, 'Burton-in-Wirral: From Domesday to Dormitory', *Cheshire History Newsletter,* No.11, (1976) pp.15-20.

12 See P.H.W.Booth, N.Mawby and M.Cullen, *Burton Church and People, A Short Guide* (Burton, 1975).

13 P.F.A.Morrell, 'The Parish Registers of the Parish of Burton', *J.C.A.S.*, N.S., XVI, (1909) pp.89-118. F.C.Beazley, 'Notes on the Parish of Burton in Wirral', *T.H.S.L.C.*, N.S., XXIII, (1907) pp.46-76.

14 K.E.Jermy, 'The Earthwork at Burton Point', *Cheshire Sheaf,* 3rd Series, Vol.55, (1960) pp.30-1. (No.10580).

15 P.H.W.Booth (ed.) *Burton-in-Wirral : A History* (Burton, 1984).

16 The standard work on Shotwick is still F.C.Beazley, 'Notes on Shotwick in the County of Chester', *T.H.S.L.C.*, N.S., XXX, (1914) pp.1-122. (reprinted with revisions, Liverpool, 1915).

17 L.Radcliffe in *Cheshire Life,* (June 1978).

18 F.H.Crossley in R.Richards, *Old Cheshire Churches* (2nd Edition, 1973) p.430.

19 W.F.Irvine, *W.N. & Q.,* Vol.2, (1893) p.6. (No.166).

20 W.F.Irvine, *W.N. & Q.,* Vol.2, (1893) pp.30-1. (No.204).

21 See Beazley, *op. cit.,* pp.51-9.

22 R.Stewart-Brown, 'The Royal Manor and Park of Shotwick in Cheshire', *T.H.S.L.C.,* XXVIII, (1912), Appendix I, pp.59-61.

23 R.Stewart-Brown, (ed.) *Accounts of the Chamberlains and other Officers of the County of Chester 1301-1360, Rec. Soc.,* Vol.LIX (1910) p.124, 129, 215.

24 Stewart-Brown, *op. cit.,* p.170.

25 See *Letters and Papers Foreign and Domestic Henry VIII,* (ed. J.Gairdner), Vol.IV, Part 2, pp.1087-8. (No.2431). E.W.Ives, 'Court and County Palatine in the Reign of Henry VIII : The Career of William Brereton of Malpas', *T.H.S.L.C.,* Vol.123, (1971) pp.31-3.

26 For example Stewart-Brown, *op. cit.,* p.215.

27 The castle was a ruin by at least the 1620's. See Webb's description (In King's *Vale Royal of England*) reproduced in *Mortimer,* Appendix, p.14.

28 *Sulley,* pp.116-7.

29 For a full description, see J.P.Rylands and F.C.Beazley, 'The Monumental and other Inscriptions in the Church of Stoak, Backford and Thornton-le-Moors in the County of Chester', *T.H.S.L.C.,* N.S., XI, (1905) pp.120-195.

30 See J.P.Earwaker, 'The Four Randle Holmes of Chester, Antiquaries, Heralds and Geneologists, c.1571 to 1707', *J.C.A.S.,* N.S., IV, (1892) pp.113-170.

31 *Ormerod,* p.388.

32 *Ormerod,* p.388. For a full description of the church architecture, see F.H.Crossley in R.Richards, *Old Cheshire Churches (2nd Edition, 1973) pp.430-2.*

33 For a full description of the Stoak panels, see Rylands and Beazley, *op. cit.,* pp.11-30. Another bell in the church is dated 1598.

34 For the early charters relating to Stanlow Abbey, see *Ormerod,* pp.400-3. The lands and gifts to the Abbey are recorded in the monastery *Coucher Book,* W.A.Hulton (ed) 3 Vols., *Chet. Soc.,* X, (1847), XI, (1847), XVI, (1848). For the agreement with the Chester monks, see J.Tait (ed.) *The Chartulary or Register of the Abbey of St. Werburgh, Chester, Chet. Soc.,* N.S., Vol.79, Part 1, (1920) pp.200-2 (No.307), pp.195-209 (No.305) et. seq.

35 M.E.Walcott, 'Inventory of Stanlow', *T.H.S.L.C.,* N.S., XII, (1871-2) pp.53-6. See also W.F.Irvine,, *W.N. & Q.,* Vol.2, (1893) pp.14-15. (No.179). E.W.Cox, *W.N. & Q.,* Vol.1, (1892) pp.67-8 (No.122) et. seq.

36 *Ormerod,* p.397.

37 E.Brotherton-Ratcliffe, 'Excavations at Grange Cow Worth, Ellesmere Port 1966 and 1967', *J.C.A.S.,* Vol.58, (1975) pp.69-80.

38 C.Platt, *The Monastic Grange in Medieval England* (New York, 1969) pp.76-93.

Chapter VII: Preserving Wirral's Past

1 See R.Strong, Foreword to P.Cormack, *Heritage in Danger* (1978) pp.10-12. R.Muir, *Shell Guide to Reading the Landscape* (1981) pp.15-17.

2 Merseyside County Council, *Merseyside Green Belt Subject Plan Written Statement* (Liverpool, 1981).

3 Cheshire County Council, *Policy for Rural Cheshire* (Chester, 1971) *The County Structure Plan : Written Statement of Policies and Proposals* (Chester, 1976). I am grateful to Mike Ross in the Cheshire County Planning Department for his help with this section.

4 Wirral Borough Council, *Wirral Planning Handbook,* (Wallasey, 1979) pp.49-51. A list of Conservation Areas in Wirral is given in Appendix I, p.149.

5 Wirral Borough Council, *Bidston Village Conservation Area Stage II Report* (Wallasey, 1976).

6 Wirral Borough Council, *Report of the Director of Development, Bidston Conservation Area* (Wallasey, 1983). I am grateful to Mr. Clark in the Wirral Borough Planning Division for access to this information, and help with listed buildings.

7 Cheshire County Council, *Conservation Stage II Report, Willaston* (Chester, 1971).

8 M.Faulkner, *An Appeal for Survival* (Birkenhead, 1971) p.1.

9 M.Wood, *The English Mediaeval House* (2nd Edition, 1965) p.xxv.

10 Wirral Borough Council, *Listed Buildings Record File, Ref.14.06.06.* Department of Environment, *List of Buildings of Special Architectural or Historic Interest, Urban District of Neston, Cheshire* (1974). Before boundary re-organisation, in 1974, part of south Wirral was included in Chester Rural District. A survey was made in 1958 and published in 1960 (Ref.1993/11/A) but this area is now under reconsideration. I would like to thank Patience Thompson, formerly with Cheshire County Council Planning Department, for letting me see her notes on the new survey of Backford and Stoak. I am grateful, too, to Oliver Bott, Conservation Officer, Cheshire County Council, for allowing me to see the provisional list for Ellesmere Port.

11 *Liverpool Daily Post,* 28 June 1978.

12 CPRE, *Planning - Friend or Foe* (1982). In 1992 the CPRE published *The Lost Land* which highlighted increasing urbanisation and loss of countryside. Copies of this report are available from CPRE, Freepost, London SWI OBR.

13 See below, Appendix II, p.150.

Listed Buildings and Conservation Areas

(1) LISTED BUILDINGS

It would be a rather unnecessary exercise to give here a comprehensive list of those buildings designated by the Department of the Environment of 'special architectural or historic interest'. All buildings built before 1700, which survive in anything like their original condition, are listed.

The statutory lists can be inspected at the Planning offices of local councils. I have included here only those buildings classed as Grade I (of outstanding interest) and Grade II * (particularly important buildings of 'special' interest). I have excluded churches.

(In Merseyside County)

GRADE I
BIRKENHEAD PRIORY (Remains), St. Mary's Gate, Birkenhead.
BRIMSTAGE HALL TOWER, Brimstage Road, Brimstage.
MARKET CROSS, Bromborough.
STORETON HALL, Lever Causeway, Storeton.

GRADE II*
BIDSTON HALL, enclosing wall and gateway to forecourt.
BIDSTON HALL, Manor Road, Birkenhead.
LEASOWE CASTLE, Leasowe Road, Wallasey.

(In Cheshire County)

GRADE II*
BARN END 'Rock Cottage,' Village Street, Burton.
LEIGHTON HALL FARM Outbuilding, Parkgate.
PUDDINGTON OLD HALL, Puddington.
SHOTWICK HALL, Shotwick.

(2) CONSERVATION AREAS

Year of designation in brackets.

(In Merseyside County)

BARNSTON (December 1983)
BIDSTON (April 1971)
BIRKENHEAD PARK (July 1977)
BROMBOROUGH (April 1982)
BROMBOROUGH POOL (October 1986)
CALDY (October 1974)
EASTHAM (April 1974)
FLAYBRICK CEMETERY, BIRKENHEAD (April 1992)
FRANKBY (October 1974)
GAYTON (April 1979)
HAMILTON SQUARE, BIRKENHEAD (July 1977)
HESWALL (LOWER VILLAGE) (April 1979)
OXTON (April 1979)
PORT SUNLIGHT (March 1978)
ROCK PARK, ROCK FERRY (February 1979)
SAUGHALL MASSIE (January 1973)
THORNTON HOUGH (April 1974)
THURSTASTON (February 1981)
WELLINGTON ROAD, NEW BRIGHTON (December 1973)
WEST KIRBY (OLD VILLAGE) (September 1973)

(In Cheshire County)

BURTON (March 1974)
ELLESMERE PORT DOCKS BASIN (December 1975)
LEDSHAM (April 1979)
NESS (March 1984)
NESTON (June 1980)
PARKGATE (April 1973)
PUDDINGTON (July 1980)
SAUGHALL (June 1982)
SHOTWICK (February 1974)
STOAK (March 1979)
WILLASTON (December 1969)

(3) SCHEDULED ANCIENT MONUMENTS

BIRKENHEAD PRIORY
BROMBOROUGH, Site of Court House.
BURTON POINT, Earthwork.
DENHALL, Chapel site, south-east of Denna Hall.
IRBY HALL
SHOTWICK CASTLE, Earthwork
STANLOW ABBEY, Remains
STORETON HALL
UPTON, Site of church, Overchurch Park.
WEST KIRBY, Grange Beacon

Source:Metropolitan Borough of Wirral, *Unitary Development Plan* (Wallasey, 1992) Department of Environment, *List of Ancient Monuments in England*, Vol.3, (7th Edition, 1978).

Appendix II

Select List of Local Societies

For an up-to-date list of Membership Secretaries etc., contact your local reference library. Most towns, and some villages, have a history or conservation society (e.g. Willaston Residents and Countryside Society).

BIRKENHEAD HISTORY SOCIETY

An active society with an informative newsletter and regular trips and talks. The society was responsible for the publication of the late Professor Allison's *Sidelights on Tranmere* (1976), an exemplary local history book.

THE BROMBOROUGH SOCIETY

Celebrated its golden jubilee in 1983, when it published an excellent commemorative booklet, *Bromborough in Times Past.*

BURTON AND SOUTH WIRRAL LOCAL HISTORY SOCIETY

More rigorous approach to local history with useful published work, largely at the direction of Paul Booth from Liverpool University.

CHESHIRE COMMUNITY COUNCIL (Local History Committee)

96 Lower Bridge Street, Chester CH1. 1RU.

Publishes the 'History of Cheshire' series of books, also the twice yearly *Cheshire History*. Responsible for history societies and historical interests in the old and new county of Cheshire.

CHESTER ARCHAEOLOGICAL SOCIETY

At one time, the Chester and North Wales Architectural, Archaelogical, and Historic Society. Not as specialised as the title suggests, although the yearly *Journal* contains articles relating to Cheshire in its widest sense.

HISTORIC SOCIETY OF LANCASHIRE AND CHESHIRE

Founded in 1848, one of the oldest and most respected local history societies. The *Transactions*, published annually, brings together scholarly articles on aspects of North West history. The Society organises lectures and conferences, and has an excellent local history collection housed at the Central Public Library in Liverpool. Members can use it for lending and reference purposes.

MERSEYSIDE ARCHAEOLOGICAL SOCIETY

Founded in 1976 to promote and support local archaeological activity and research at both professional and voluntary level. From this, the Archaeological Survey of Merseyside developed and the Society publishes the results of the Survey's excavations.

THE WIRRAL SOCIETY

Founded in 1928 and affiliated to the Council for the Protection of Rural England. The booklet *Wirral – Yesterday, Today and Tomorrow*, published to commemorate the Society's golden jubilee in 1978, outlines their aims and the publication '*The Wirral Society...60 Years On*' (1988) develops some of their themes. The Executive Commitee consider planning proposals and threats to Wirral's Green Belt and work closely with other interested parties, notably -

WIRRAL FOOTPATHS AND OPEN SPACES PRESERVATION SOCIETY

WIRRAL GREEN BELT COUNCIL

Appendix III
The Search for Local History

Invariably, the search for local history begins at the reference library. Wallasey Central, (Earlston Road, Wallasey), and Birkenhead Central, (Borough Road, Birkenhead), have the main secondary works about Wirral and also useful newspaper cuttings and off-prints of relevant articles. The Central Public Library (William Brown Street, Liverpool), has an excellent collection of local history material including that of the Historic Society of Lancashire and Cheshire.

B.E.Harris (ed.), *The History of the County Palatine of Chester: A Short Bibliography and Guide to Sources*, (Chester, 1983), is the most recent survey of literature relating to Wirral and Cheshire.

For old buildings and sites, a visit to the *Sites and Monuments Record* at Liverpool Museum, (William Brown Street, Liverpool), is essential. This survey was set up in 1978 and gives very full references for the Metropolitan Borough of Wirral. The Merseyside Archaeological Society publication, *Handbook 1 : Recording the Evidence*, (Liverpool, 1978), will be useful.

A similar archaeological record for the Cheshire County part of Wirral exists at the County Planning Department, (Cheshire County Council, Commerce House, Hunter Street, Chester).

For the student of local history, the books by W.G.Hoskins form an excellent starting point; in particular, *The Making of the English Landscape,* (9th edition, Harmonsworth, 1970), *Local History in England,* (2nd edition, 1972), and *Fieldwork in Local History*, (2nd edition, 1982). The books by David Iredale, *Enjoying Archives,* (Chichester, 1980), and *Local History Research and Writing* (Chichester, 1980), are also useful.

The Historical Association (59a Kennington Park Road, London SE11 4JH), publish a number of pamphlets to assist local historians and especially useful is the *Local History Handlist* (5th edition, 1979) — a very complete bibliography and guide to sources.

Another invaluable aid is *The Local Historian's Encyclopedia* by John Richardson (New Barnet, 1974, reprint, 1981). This has been described as 'probably the most useful book for the working local historian ever published' and covers archives, archaeology and many other relevant subjects. W.B.Stephens, *Sources for English Local History* (1973) is also essential reading. P.Cunnington, *How Old is Your House?* (Revised ed., 1982) is good for architectural history and interpretation. The 'Discovering' series published by Shire contains some useful guides.

The following survey of possible research areas is of necessity rather brief, but I hope it will assist in your own search for old Wirral.

Early maps are particularly valuable, especially when they show changed or changing features of the landscape. Perhaps the best known early work is that of John Speed, published in 1611, which shows towns, villages, churches, hills, parks, trees and windmills. The first map of Cheshire on a large scale was published in 1777 by Peter P.Burdett (Facsimile edition : Historic Society of Lancashire and Cheshire, occasional series, No.1, 1974).

The first Ordnance Survey map of the country, at a scale of one inch to one mile, was published in the years 1833-43. W.G.Hoskins has described the O.S. map as 'the most rewarding single document we could have for the study of English topography'.

Tithe maps show a town or village as it was in the 1840's and usually give all the owners and occupiers of the land, and field names. Field names are frequently indicative of former land usage. These maps are held in the Cheshire Record Office, (Duke Street, Chester CH1 1RL).

For further information on early maps, see J.B.Harley, 'Maps for the Local Historian : A Guide to the British Sources', (reprinted from *The Local Historian*, 1972), C.Moore, *Old Maps of Cheshire*, (Tarporley, 1981) and H.Whittaker, *A Descriptive*

List of the Printed Maps of Cheshire, 1577-1900, (Chetham Society, 2nd Series, Vol.106, 1942).

The County Record Office at Chester will also give access to a multitude of original documents relating to Wirral; wills, inventories, court proceeedings etc. However, a knowledge of Latin and a grasp of palaeography is often essential. See the *Cheshire Record Office Guide* (1991).

The *Domesday Book* is now available in an excellent modern edition, (see Bibliography), and is a good introduction to mediaeval Wirral. Mediaeval cartularies, or registers, record grants of land made to a particular religious foundation. The register relating to the Abbey of St. Werburgh has been published by the Chetham Society (edited by J.Tait, 2 volumes, N.S., Vol.79, 1920, Vol.82, 1923).

Of the other ecclesiastical records, parish registers are raw material for population study and snippets of social history. Several have been transcribed for Wirral, and a visit to the Cheshire Record Office will tell you what is available.

Further avenues of approach include air photographs — which may reveal old field patterns or habitation — and hedge counting which is based upon the assumption that a hedge will contain one shrub species for every hundred years of life. While this theory is straightforward enough, the practice of hedge-counting does require some expertise in flora identification. Both aerial archaeology, and hedge-counting, should always be carried out in conjunction with documentary evidence.

The study and pursuit of local history can be enhanced by attending the many educational classes held in Wirral, or Merseyside generally. The University of Liverpool Institute of Extension Studies, (1 Abercromby Square, P.O. Box 147, Liverpool L69 3BX), runs a three year part-time *Diploma in Local History* (which began in 1974) under the guidance of Paul Booth. The Institute also offers several other courses, sometimes in alliance with the Workers Educational Association (WEA). In the 1983-4 session these included 'The Archaeology of Wirral and Britain AD 400-1000 : An Introduction', 'The Wyldrenesse of Wyrale : Wirral and Cheshire in the Middle Ages' and 'Introduction to Local History'.

No previous experience is necessary for the WEA courses which often give an excellent grounding in historical and archaeological techniques. Possibly less rigorous are those local interest courses organised by Wirral Metropolitan College (Adult Education Unit, Withens Lane, Wallasey, Merseyside L45 7LT).

Chester College of Higher Education, (Cheyney Road, Chester CH1 4BJ), occasionally offers a three year part-time *Diploma in Landscape History* which traces the making of the English landscape - both urban and rural - from prehistoric to modern times.

The *Merseyside Records Users Group* aims to facilitate research work and can be contacted at the Department of History, University of Liverpool.

Finally, of the local museums, the Williamson Art Gallery and Museum (Slatey Road, Birkenhead) has expanded its local history section and several exhibitions have been mounted. In 1988 the undercroft at Birkenhead Priory was opened as an exhibition centre for the display of the priory's history and associated artefacts. There are plans for a permanent Wirral Museum based at Birkenhead Town Hall.

The Grosvenor Museum, (Grosvenor Street, Chester), has no Wirral antiquities on permanent display, but the Meols finds can be viewed by appointment. Liverpool Museum (William Brown Street, Liverpool), also has a collection of Meols artefacts. In 1983 they mounted an exhibition, 'A Future for the Past', which highlighted the work of the Archaeological Survey of Merseyside and some of their techniques of rescue and restoration. (This Survey was established in 1977 and is funded partly by the Department of the Environment and partly by the University of Liverpool).

Select Bibliography

There has been no shortage of books and articles about Wirral. Most of our present knowledge derives from the labours of a number of distinguished local historians who flourished in the first half of the twentieth-century. Among them were W.F.Irvine, J.Brownbill, F.C.Beazley and R.Stewart-Brown and many of their articles appeared in the Transactions of the Historic Society of Lancashire and Cheshire.

The standard reference work for Wirral history has long been Volume 2 of G.Ormerod's *The History of the County Palatine and City of Chester* (2nd edition, revised and enlarged by T.Helsby, 1882). Ormerod followed the fashions of his age, with a massive tome of seemingly endless detail based on many early charters and family papers. He is excellent for heraldry and genealogy, not so good for architecture, social and economic matters.

The History of the Hundred of Wirral, with a Sketch of the City and County of Chester by W.W.Mortimer (1847, republished by E.J.Morten, Manchester, 1972) is in some respects a more condensed version of Ormerod, with a lengthy historical introduction. Philip Sulley's book, *The Hundred of Wirral* (Birkenhead, 1889), adds little new information but, like many old histories, is useful for descriptions of buildings that have been lost or radically altered.

More recently, Wirral has attracted the sort of antiquarian-cum-naturalist type of book epitomised by Norman Ellison's *The Wirral Peninsula* (1955). Ellison's book reflects a genuine love and grasp of subject, and he followed a long local tradition of books like Hilda Gamlin's *'Twixt Mersey and Dee* (Liverpool, 1897) and Henry Young's *A Perambulation of the Hundred of Wirral* (Liverpool, 1909).

In the 1980's, with so many changes — not least in buildings and boundaries — Ellison's classic work was in need of some revision. Kenneth Burnley was entrusted with this task and *Portrait of Wirral* (1981), is a comprehensive although somewhat lack-lustre account. Eminently more readable and anecdotal is Alan Brack's *The Wirral,* published in 1980.

Wirral really requires a definitive general history book, absorbing the results of modern research and placing the peninsula in the context of county and national events. Recent 'serious' studies have been rather specialised, so we have, for example, excellent although microsmic works on Burton and Hilbre Island. The 'Wirral' volume of *The Victoria County History of Chester* (ed. B.E.Harris, 1979 onward) may go some way in achieving this 'over-view'.

The Victoria History is rather academic, but perhaps the most reliable general study of Cheshire and work is still in progress. Four general volumes will be followed by various regional studies; Vol.2 (1979) covers administration and forests, Vol.3 (1980) religion and education and Volume 1 (1987) prehistory, the Romans, Anglo-Saxons, and the Domesday Survey.

Wirral also features in a series of well-produced and accessible studies published by The Cheshire Community Council. *A History of Cheshire,* (ed. J.J.Bagley, Chester 1964 onward), is an admirable project although some of the material is badly in need of revision, in the light of more recent research. Dorothy Sylvester's *A History of Cheshire* (2nd edition, Chichester, 1980) is another good general survey with many illustrations.

R.N.Dore's chapter in *Cheshire* (1976), is an excellent synthesis and there is a chapter on Wirral in David Bethell's *Portrait of Cheshire* (1980).

For architecture, the standard guide is Nikolaus Pevsner and Edward Hubbard, *The Buildings of England : Cheshire* (Harmondsworth, 1971) while R.W.Brunskill, *Traditional Buildings of Britain* (1981) and R.Foster, *Discovering English Churches* (1981) will lead to a greater understanding of architectural styles. For a list of terms, see J.Harris and J.Lever, *Illustrated Glossary of Architecture 850-1830* (1969 edition).

Much Wirral history is tucked away in learned journals and magazines. My own debt to the *Transactions* of the Historic Society of Lancashire and Cheshire, (1849 onward), is obvious. The Transactions are published annually and available to members by subscription. (See Appendix II). The Cheshire Community Council publishes the twice yearly Cheshire History, (1978 onward), also available by subscription. (See Appendix II).

There is an enormous amount of original material relating to Wirral contained in *The Cheshire Sheaf* (1878 onward) which originally appeared as a series of short articles in the Chester Courant, the Cheshire Observer, and the Deesider. Similarly, *Wirral Notes and Queries* (ed. F.Sanders and W.F.Irvine, 2 vols, Birkenhead, 1892-3) is a mine of information and first appeared as a series of short articles in the Birkenhead News.

The Wirral Journal (1982 onward) is published quarterly and deserves a mention. Although not strictly historical, and only rarely innovatory, it brings together a variety of local interest topics in a very readable format. It is an excellent publicity exercise for the peninsula, and Kenneth Burnley must be congratulated for this.

The following list of books relating to individual chapters are those which I have found particularly useful, and are either in print or easily accessible. Detailed references to the statements in the text will be found in the notes to each chapter.

CHAPTER I
J.Beck, *Tudor Cheshire* (Chester, 1969).
R.W.Brunskill, *Illustrated Handbook of Vernacular Architecture* (1971).
J.D.Bu'Lock, *Pre-Conquest Cheshire 383-1066* (Chester, 1972).
G.Chitty, 'Wirral Rural Fringes Survey', *Journal of the Merseyside Archaeological Society,* Vol.2, (Liverpool, 1978 ; reprint, 1980).
J.T.Driver, *Cheshire in the Later Middle Ages* (Chester, 1971).
R.Foster, *Discovering English Churches* (1981).
B.E.Harris (ed.),*Victoria History of Cheshire,* Vol.II (1979), Vol.III (1980).
W.Hewitt, *The Wirral Peninsula* (Liverpool, 1922).
B.M.C.Husain, *Cheshire under the Norman Earls* (Chester, 1973).
J.McN.Dodgson, *The Place-Names of Cheshire,* Part IV (English Place-Name Society, Vol.XLVII, Cambridge, 1972).
P.Morgan (ed.) *Domesday Book : Cheshire, including Lancashire, Cumbria, and North Wales* (Chichester, 1978).
R.Richards, *Old Cheshire Churches* (2nd Edition, 1973).

CHAPTER II
A.Hume, *Ancient Meols* (1863).
E.C.Woods and P.C.Brown, *The Rise and Progress of Wallasey* (3rd Edition, Wallasey, 1974).

CHAPTER III
J.E.Allison, *Sidelights on Tranmere* (Birkenhead, 1976).
G.Chitty et al., *Bromborough Court House : A Survey of the Evidence,* Merseyside Archaeological Society, Report 2, (Liverpool, 1979).
R.Stewart-Brown, *Birkenhead Priory and the Mersey Ferry* (Liverpool, 1925).

CHAPTER IV & V
J.Brownbill, *West Kirby and Hilbre* (Liverpool, 1928).

CHAPTER VI
J.D.Craggs (ed.) *Hilbre, the Cheshire Island* (Liverpool, 1982).

CHAPTER VII
O.Bott and R.Williams, *Man's Imprint on Cheshire* (Chester, 1975).
Cheshire County Council, *Cheshire Your Heritage* (2nd Edition, Chester, 1977).
P.Cormack, *Heritage in Danger* (1978).
R.Muir, *Shell Guide to Reading the Landscape* (1981).

121.
Ince Manor House (The only surviving mediaeval manor house belonging to the Abbot of Chester).

Index

Main references in the text are indicated in bold type.